A BALANCED MATHEMATICS PROGRAM INTEGRATING SCIENCE AND LANGUAGE ARTS

Unit Resource Guide
Unit 12
Dissections

THIRD EDITION

KENDALL/HUNT PUBLISHING COMPANY
4050 Westmark Drive   Dubuque, Iowa 52002

A TIMS® Curriculum
University of Illinois at Chicago

UIC The University of Illinois
at Chicago

The original edition was based on work supported by the National Science Foundation under grant No. MDR 9050226 and the University of Illinois at Chicago. Any opinions, findings, and conclusions or recommendations expressed in this publication are those of the author(s) and do not necessarily reflect the views of the granting agencies.

Letter Home

Dissections

Date: _____

Dear Family Member:

In this unit, *Dissections,* we take things apart to learn about them. Once something is taken apart, getting it back together can be a problem. Students use a set of seven shapes to solve puzzles called tangrams. Although one aim is to have fun solving geometric puzzles, there are also mathematical goals. Through making, drawing, and describing geometric shapes, students develop spatial visualization skills and the ability to think abstractly. Working the puzzles develops geometric problem-solving skills. Communication and logical thinking skills are required when students share their solutions or explain why certain problems have no solutions. Area, perimeter, angle size, symmetry, definition, classification, and congruence are other important geometric ideas that students will encounter. The unit also includes gathering and organizing data and carrying out systematic searches.

The seven tans of tangrams—an old Chinese puzzle

- **Describing Shapes.** Help your child by asking him or her to identify shapes at home and to discuss the parts of common geometric shapes. Talking about the number of sides and corners of various shapes—triangles, squares, pentagons, and so on—is worthwhile. You might also make a list of examples of right angles—square corners—at home. Comparing angles to see if they are more or less than a right angle will help your child understand angular measure.

- **Math Facts.** Help your child study the multiplication facts for the twos and threes using *Triangle Flash Cards.*

Thank you for taking time to talk with your child about math.

Sincerely,

_____

Carta al hogar

Disecciones

Fecha: _____

Estimado miembro de familia:

En esta unidad, *Disecciones,* desarmamos cosas para aprender acerca de ellas. Una vez que desarmamos alguna cosa, volver a armarla puede ser un problema. Los estudiantes tendrán un conjunto de siete figuras para armar rompecabezas llamado tangrama. Aunque uno de los objetivos es divertirse resolviendo rompecabezas geométricos, también hay objetivos matemáticos. A través de la práctica, los dibujos y la descripción de figuras geométricas, los estudiantes desarrollan habilidades de visualización espacial y la habilidad para pensar en forma abstracta. Armar rompecabezas desarrolla las habilidades para resolver problemas geométricos. También se requiere el uso de las habilidades comunicativas y de pensamiento lógico cuando los estudiantes comparten sus soluciones o explican por qué ciertos problemas no tienen solución. Otras ideas geométricas importantes con las que los estudiantes se encontrarán son el área, el perímetro, la medida de los ángulos, la simetría, la definición, la clasificación y la congruencia. En esta unidad también se reúnen y organizan datos y se realizan búsquedas sistemáticas.

Los siete tans de un tangrama, un antiguo rompecabezas chino

- **Describir figuras.** Ayude a su hijo/a pidiéndole que identifique figuras en casa y hablen sobre las partes de figuras geométricas comunes. Es muy útil hablar acerca del número de lados y esquinas de distintas figuras (triángulos, cuadrados, pentágonos, etc.). También pueden hacer una lista con ejemplos de ángulos rectos que encuentren en casa, por ejemplo, esquinas cuadradas. Comparar ángulos para ver si son más grandes o más pequeños que un ángulo recto ayudará a su hijo/a a comprender el concepto de la medida de los ángulos.

- **Conceptos básicos.** Ayude a su hijo/a a estudiar las tablas de multiplicación del dos y del tres usando las tarjetas triangulares.

Gracias por tomarse el tiempo para hablar con su hijo/a acerca de las matemáticas.

Atentamente,

_____

Table of Contents

Unit 12
Dissections

Unit 12

Outline
Dissections

Unit Summary

Students make, draw, measure, describe, and analyze plane geometric figures. Much of the work involves figures that can be made with small sets of constituent pieces; we say the figures are "dissected" into the pieces. In the first activity, students use Tangrams to solve puzzles and create shapes. In *Building with Triangles,* students build plane geometric shapes with triangles and then investigate congruence, transformations (turns and flips), area, perimeter, and symmetry. They study relationships between attributes of shapes (e.g., the number of sides and the number of corners). As culminating activities, students solve geometric puzzles and play a geometric game similar to tic-tac-toe. The DPP for this unit provides practice with and assesses the multiplication facts for the 2s and 3s.

Major Concept Focus

- multiple representations of shapes
- naming two-dimensional shapes
- spatial visualization skills
- analyzing shapes
- measuring area in square inches
- measuring perimeter in centimeters
- congruence
- sides
- corners (vertices)
- angles
- right angles
- flips
- turns
- line symmetry
- Game: geometric game requiring logical reasoning
- practice and assessment of the multiplication facts for the 2s and 3s

Pacing Suggestions

Lesson 6 *Focus on Word Problems* is an optional lesson. These problems can be solved in class or assigned as homework throughout the unit. Since the lesson requires little teacher preparation, it is appropriate for a substitute teacher.

Assessment Indicators

Use the following Assessment Indicators and the *Observational Assessment Record* that follows the Background section in this unit to assess students on key ideas.

A1. Can students analyze and describe 2-dimensional shapes using their properties (number of sides, corners, and right angles)?

A2. Can students measure area and perimeter of 2-dimensional shapes?

A3. Can students identify congruent shapes?

A4. Can students identify line symmetry?

A5. Can students use geometric concepts and skills to solve problems and communicate their reasoning?

A6. Do students demonstrate fluency for the multiplication facts for the 2s and 3s?

Unit Planner

	Lesson Information	Supplies	Copies/Transparencies

Lesson 1

Tangrams

URG Pages 21–38
SG Pages 158–165
DAB Page 185

DPP A–D
HP Part 1

Estimated Class Sessions
2

Activity
Students explore tangram puzzles—those in which pieces are joined edge to edge. Students solve several puzzles, discuss why others are unsolvable, and design their own puzzles.

Math Facts
DPP Bit A introduces the *Triangle Flash Cards: 2s* and *3s*. Bit C provides practice with the twos.

Homework
1. Assign Home Practice Part 1.
2. Have students share the puzzle they made on the *Making a Tangram Puzzle* Activity Page with a family member.
3. Assign some of the problems in the Puzzling Tangrams section of the *Tangrams* Activity Pages in the *Student Guide*.
4. Remind students to take home their *Triangle Flash Cards* to study with a family member.

Assessment
Use the Journal Prompt as an assessment.

Supplies
- 1 set of tangram pieces per student
- 1 envelope for storing tangram pieces per student
- 1 envelope for storing flash cards per student
- 1 ruler per student

Copies/Transparencies
- 1 copy of *Tangram Pieces Master* URG Page 32 per student pair, optional
- 1 transparency of *Hints for Puzzling Tangrams* URG Page 33

Lesson 2

Building with Triangles

URG Pages 39–56
SG Pages 166–169
DAB Pages 187–188

DPP E–F
HP Part 2

Estimated Class Sessions
1-2

Activity
Students make shapes by putting two or three isosceles right triangles together edge to edge. They trace shapes on paper and measure, describe, and analyze them.

Homework
1. Assign the Building with Three Triangles section for homework.
2. Assign Home Practice Part 2.

Assessment
1. During the activity observe students' abilities to identify right angles, recognize congruent shapes, show lines of symmetry, and measure area and perimeter. Record your observations on the *Observational Assessment Record*.
2. Use the Journal Prompt to assess students' abilities to explain their reasoning.

Supplies
- 1 pair of scissors per student
- 1 centimeter ruler per student
- 1 envelope for storing triangles per student group
- markers or crayons
- 3 small triangles from 2 tangram sets per student group
- 1 square from a set of tangrams, optional per student group

Copies/Transparencies
- 1 copy of *Lines of Symmetry* URG Page 51 per student, optional
- 1 or 2 copies of *Right Triangle Master* URG Page 52 on heavy paper, optional
- 1 transparency of *When Are Shapes the Same?* URG Page 53
- 1 copy of *Observational Assessment Record* URG Pages 11–12 to be used throughout this unit

Lesson 3

Building with Four Triangles

URG Pages 57–73
SG Pages 170–172

DPP G–J
HP Part 3

Estimated Class Sessions
2

Activity
This activity extends the previous activity. Students investigate shapes they can make by putting together four isosceles right triangles edge to edge.

Math Facts
For item J, students illustrate multiplication number sentences.

Homework
1. Assign some of Professor Peabody's Shape Riddles.
2. Assign Home Practice Part 3.

Assessment
Students complete the *Three Tans* Assessment Pages.

Supplies
- 1 pair of scissors per student
- 1 centimeter ruler per student
- plain paper to sketch shapes
- 1 envelope for storing cutout shapes per student group
- 2 sets of tangrams per student group

Copies/Transparencies
- 1 copy of *Four Triangles Data Tables 1* and *2* URG Pages 65–66 per student group, optional
- 1 copy of *Tangram Pieces Master* URG Page 32 per student group, optional
- 1 copy of *Three Tans* URG Pages 67–68 per student
- 1 transparency of *Four Triangles Data Tables 1* and *2* URG Pages 65–66
- 1 transparency of *Tangram Pieces Master* URG Page 32, colored and cut out or 2 sets of tangram pieces

	Lesson Information	Supplies	Copies/Transparencies
Lesson 4 **Dissection Puzzles** URG Pages 74–83 SG Pages 173–175 DAB Page 189 DPP K–L HP Part 4 *Estimated Class Sessions* **1**	**Activity** Students solve puzzles that require dissecting figures in specific ways. In each puzzle, they put together a set of pieces edge to edge to make various shapes. **Math Facts** DPP Bit K provides practice with the multiplication facts for the threes. **Homework** 1. Puzzles may be assigned for homework. 2. Assign Home Practice Part 4. **Assessment** 1. Puzzle C provides an opportunity to observe students' abilities to analyze and describe two-dimensional shapes. Record your observations on the *Observational Assessment Record*. 2. Transfer information from the Unit 12 *Observational Assessment Record* to students' *Individual Assessment Record Sheets*.	• 1 pair of scissors per student • 1 set of tangram pieces per student, optional	• 1 copy of *Individual Assessment Record Sheet* TIG Assessment section per student, previously copied for use throughout the year
Lesson 5 **Hex** URG Pages 84–89 DAB Page 191 DPP M–N *Estimated Class Sessions* **1**	**Game** Students play a geometric game similar to tic-tac-toe or "boxes." Later, this game will be adapted to provide practice in estimation and mental computation. **Math Facts** DPP Bit M is a quiz on the twos and threes multiplication facts. **Homework** 1. Encourage students to play *Hex* with a family member. 2. Assign the word problems in Lesson 6 for homework. **Assessment** DPP Bit M is a quiz to assess the twos and threes multiplication facts.	• 25 of each of 2 kinds of beans or other small markers per student pair	• 1 transparency of *4-by-4 Hex* URG Page 89, optional
Lesson 6 **Focus on Word Problems** URG Pages 90–96 SG Pages 176–177 *Estimated Class Sessions* **1**	OPTIONAL LESSON **Optional Activity** Students solve problems that involve addition, subtraction, multiplication, or division. **Homework** Assign some or all of the problems for homework.	• 1 ruler per student	• 1 copy of *Centimeter Graph Paper* URG Page 94 per student

Connections

A current list of literature and software connections is available at *www.mathtrailblazers.com*. You can also find information on connections in the *Teacher Implementation Guide* Literature List and Software List sections.

Literature Connections

Suggested Titles

- Burns, Marilyn. *The Greedy Triangle.* Scholastic Press, Inc., New York, 1995.
- Maccarone, Grace. *Three Pigs, One Wolf & Seven Magic Shapes.* Scholastic Press, Inc., New York, 1998.
- Pilegard, Virginia Walton. *The Warlord's Puzzle.* Pelican Publishing Company, Gretna, LA, 2000.
- Tompert, Ann. *Grandfather Tang's Story.* Dragonfly Books, Cambridgeshire, UK, 1997. (Lesson 1)

Software Connections

- *Math Munchers Deluxe* provides practice in basic facts, angles, and identifying geometric shapes in an arcade-like game.
- *National Library of Virtual Manipulatives* website (http://matti.usu.edu) allows students to work with manipulatives including geoboards and tangrams.
- *Shape Up!* is a geometry program that contains five sets of shapes that students can manipulate and explore.

Teaching All Math Trailblazers Students

Math Trailblazers® lessons are designed for students with a wide range of abilities. The lessons are flexible and do not require significant adaptation for diverse learning styles or academic levels. However, when needed, lessons can be tailored to allow students to engage their abilities to the greatest extent possible while building knowledge and skills.

To assist you in meeting the needs of all students in your classroom, this section contains information about some of the features in the curriculum that allow all students access to mathematics. For additional information, see the Teaching the *Math Trailblazers* Student: Meeting Individual Needs section in the *Teacher Implementation Guide.*

Differentiation Opportunities in this Unit

Games

Use games to promote or extend understanding of math concepts and to practice skills with children who need more practice.

- Lesson 5 *Hex*

DPP Challenges

DPP Challenges are items from the Daily Practice and Problems that usually take more than fifteen minutes to complete. These problems are more thought-provoking and can be used to stretch students' problem-solving skills. The following lesson has a DPP Challenge in it:

- DPP Challenge N from Lesson 5 *Hex*

Journal Prompts

Journal prompts provide opportunities for students to explain and reflect on mathematical problems. They can help both students who need practice explaining their ideas and students who benefit from answering higher order questions. Students with various learning styles can express themselves using pictures, words, and sentences. Teachers can alter journal prompts to suit students' ability levels. The following lessons contain a journal prompt:

- Lesson 1 *Tangrams*
- Lesson 2 *Building with Triangles*
- Lesson 3 *Building with Four Triangles*
- Lesson 4 *Dissection Puzzles*

Extensions

Use extensions to enrich lessons. Many extensions provide opportunities to further involve or challenge students of all abilities. Take a moment to review the extensions prior to beginning this unit. Some extensions may require additional preparation and planning. The following lessons contain extensions:

- Lesson 1 *Tangrams*
- Lesson 4 *Dissection Puzzles*
- Lesson 5 *Hex*
- Lesson 6 *Focus on Word Problems*

Unit 12

Background
Dissections

Taking something apart—dissecting it—is a good way to learn about it. We learn what the parts are, how they fit together, and how they relate to one another. Whether we want to learn about frogs, car engines, or squares, taking our subject apart is a good beginning.

Once a thing is taken apart, however, getting it back together may be problematic. Our unit begins with a series of such problems: What figures can be made with a given set of pieces? In the first lesson students make shapes with the seven tangram pieces. In the next two activities, *Building with Triangles* and *Building with Four Triangles,* the pieces are isosceles right triangles. In these three activities, the pieces must be joined edge to edge. This restriction may inhibit artistry, but it increases the mathematical content. The unit also includes *Dissection Puzzles,* a game, *Hex,* and a set of word problems.

School Geometry: Holistic to Analytic

Many students perceive geometric shapes as undifferentiated wholes. They recognize squares and triangles, and may even be able to use terms like *rhombus* or *trapezoid;* but they are probably not aware of the parts of those shapes or of relationships between those parts. Such students do not realize that a square has four sides and four corners or that the angles are right angles and the sides are equal. They know a triangle is not a square, but cannot compare and contrast the two shapes; they do not discriminate the parts of the geometric whole. We may say that such students view shapes holistically.

A more advanced understanding requires discerning the parts of shapes and recognizing relationships among those parts. Drawing, measuring,

and describing shapes can help develop this understanding. So also can breaking shapes down into their components and analyzing them so that their parts and properties are explicit—our word *analysis* comes from the Greek for "a breaking up." Developing this more analytic understanding is the key aim of this unit.

The levels of geometric understanding—and several more advanced stages—were first identified in the late 1950s by two Dutch mathematics educators, Pierre M. van Hiele and Dina van Hiele-Geldof. Mary Crowley discusses this in her article "The van Hiele Model of the Development of Geometric Thought." (See *Resources.*)

Dissections

A **dissection** is literally a cutting into pieces. In mathematics, the things being cut into pieces are usually geometric figures. This unit focuses on dissections of plane (two-dimensional) figures.

Dissections are a rich source of puzzles. Jigsaw puzzles are a kind of dissection, although not a very mathematical one. Tangram puzzles are also dissections, again not necessarily mathematical unless certain restrictions are imposed.

The classic dissection puzzle requires rearranging pieces from one shape to make another shape. Usually, a solution that uses fewer pieces is considered more elegant. Figure 1 shows such a puzzle: Can you cut the square into two pieces that exactly cover the triangle?

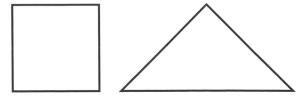

Figure 1: *A dissection puzzle*

Such puzzles can be extremely challenging. For example, can you dissect the square in Figure 2 so that the pieces exactly cover the irregular hexagon?

Figure 2: *A harder dissection puzzle*

The dissections in this unit, fortunately, are not nearly as hard as this one. A good puzzle, however, should be challenging, or it's no fun.

Words, Words, Words

Vocabulary boosting is not a major goal of *Math Trailblazers,* but effective communication is, and words are important for that. Too often, traditional mathematics texts turn geometry into a dreary parade of terms and definitions. Appropriate terminology can enhance both communication and understanding; children also enjoy learning and using fancy words. The issue is balance; use your professional judgment.

The Key Vocabulary section in the Lesson Guides lists minimal requirements. We cannot, for example, imagine talking about the parts of a triangle unless *side* and *corner* are understood. Other technical terms are used in the lessons—for example, hexagon, trapezoid, quadrilateral—but are not as critical. We leave to your discretion the degree of familiarity you want your students to have with such terms.

When you talk about vocabulary with your students, distinguish mathematical English from everyday English. In mathematics, we often seize upon everyday terms and give them precise meanings that may differ from common meanings.

Then, ironically, we complain loudly when the terms are used in their everyday sense. In everyday language, for example, a square is not a rectangle—it's a square. For most people, "rectangle" means "nonsquare rectangle." When we insist that "A square is a rectangle," students who are thinking only of vernacular meanings may conclude that mathematics is nonsense. By distinguishing mathematical usage from everyday usage, you may avoid this outcome.

Remember also that communication is more than vocabulary. Several times in this unit, for example, students are asked to explain how they know that all shapes that can be made with a given number of triangles have been identified. At other times, students are asked to describe how they solved a problem. Effective mathematical communication includes clearly describing procedures and results and arguing convincingly.

Tangrams and the Edge-to-Edge Rule

Tangram puzzles are quite popular. The majority of tangram designs are renderings of animals, flowers, people, or other real objects. In most tangram puzzles, the only rules for making shapes is that the tangram pieces must touch without overlapping. In some activities in this unit we introduce another rule, the "edge-to-edge" rule. This rule requires that the edge of one tangram piece exactly match the edge of the adjacent tangram piece. This restriction limits the space needed to work with the tangram pieces and makes problems more interesting and manageable.

Some popular literature on tangrams states they were invented thousands of years ago. This is probably untrue. It is likely they are only a few hundred years old, not a few thousand. (On the other hand, magic squares, introduced in Unit 2, *Strategies: An Assessment Unit,* really are ancient.)

Resources

- Coffin, Stewart T. *The Puzzling World of Polyhedral Dissections.* Oxford University Press, Oxford, 1990.
- Crowley, Mary L. "The van Hiele Model of the Development of Geometric Thought." In Mary M. Lindquist (Ed.), *Learning and Teaching Geometry, K–12: 1987 Yearbook.* The National Council of Teachers of Mathematics, Reston, VA.
- Dudeney, Henry E. *Amusements in Mathematics.* Dover Publications, New York, 1970.
- Gardner, Martin. *The 2nd Scientific American Book of Mathematical Puzzles and Diversions.* University of Chicago Press, Chicago, IL, 1987.
- Loyd, Sam, and Peter Van Note (Ed.). *The 8th Book of Tan: 700 Tangrams.* Dover Publications, New York, 1968.
- Read, Ronald C. *Tangrams—330 Puzzles.* Dover Publications, New York, 1980.
- Slocum, Jerry, and Jack Botermans. *Puzzles Old and New: How to Make and Solve Them.* University of Washington Press, Seattle, 1986.

Observational Assessment Record

A1 Can students analyze and describe 2-dimensional shapes using their properties (number of sides, corners, and right angles)?

A2 Can students measure area and perimeter of 2-dimensional shapes?

A3 Can students identify congruent shapes?

A4 Can students identify line symmetry?

A5 Can students use geometric concepts and skills to solve problems and communicate their reasoning?

A6 Do students demonstrate fluency for the multiplication facts for the 2s and 3s?

A7 _____

Name	A1	A2	A3	A4	A5	A6	A7	Comments
1.								
2.								
3.								
4.								
5.								
6.								
7.								
8.								
9.								
10.								
11.								
12.								
13.								

Name	A1	A2	A3	A4	A5	A6	A7	Comments
14.								
15.								
16.								
17.								
18.								
19.								
20.								
21.								
22.								
23.								
24.								
25.								
26.								
27.								
28.								
29.								
30.								
31.								
32.								

Unit 12

Daily Practice and Problems
Dissections

N Number Sense	Computation	Time	Geometry
F, J	E–H, J	I	B, D, L, N

Math Facts	$ Money	Measurement	Data
A, C, J, K, M	F	N	

Practicing and Assessing the Multiplication Facts

By the end of third grade, students are expected to demonstrate fluency with the multiplication facts. In Units 3–10, students explored patterns in multiplication and developed strategies for learning the multiplication facts. In this unit, they study the twos and threes.

DPP Bit A introduces the *Triangle Flash Cards: 2s and 3s*. Flash cards are in the *Discovery Assignment Book* immediately following the Home Practice. In Unit 12, DPP items C, J, and K provide practice with multiplication facts in these groups and Bit M is a quiz.

For information on the study of the multiplication facts in Grade 3, see the DPP Guide for Unit 3. For a detailed explanation of our approach to learning and assessing the math facts in Grade 3, see the *Grade 3 Facts Resource Guide* and for information for Grades K–5, see the TIMS Tutor: *Math Facts* in the *Teacher Implementation Guide*.

 **Daily Practice and Problems**

Students may solve the items individually, in groups, or as a class. The items may also be assigned for homework. The DPPs are also available on the Teacher Resource CD.

Student Questions	Teacher Notes

 Triangle Flash Cards: 2s and 3s

With a partner, use your *Triangle Flash Cards* to quiz each other on the multiplication facts for the twos and threes. One partner covers the corner containing the highest number. This number will be the product. The second person multiplies the two uncovered numbers.

Separate the used cards into three piles: those facts you know and can answer quickly, those you can figure out with a strategy, and those you need to learn. Practice the last two piles again and then make a list of the facts you need to practice at home for homework.

Circle the facts you know and can answer quickly on your *Multiplication Facts I Know* chart.

TIMS Bit

The *Triangle Flash Cards* follow the Home Practice for this unit in the *Discovery Assignment Book.* Remind students to take home the list of the facts they need to practice and their *Triangle Flash Cards* to study with a family member.

Have students record the facts they know well on their *Multiplication Facts I Know* charts. Students should circle the facts they know and can answer quickly. Since these charts can also be used as multiplication tables, students should have them available to use as needed.

Inform students when you will give the quiz on the 2s and 3s. This quiz appears in TIMS Bit M.

Right Angles 1

1. How many right (square) angles do you see inside the shapes below? Circle them as you count.

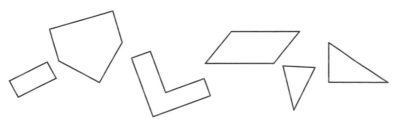

2. Tell how you decided which angles were right angles.

TIMS Task

1. the rectangle (4), pentagon (3), hexagon (5), right triangle (1); total is 13

2. Answers will vary. Examples: "I used the corner of my ruler." "I used the corner of a sheet of paper.

 Using Twos

Do these problems in your head. Write only the answers.

A. $2 \times 9 =$　　　　B. $3 \times 20 =$

C. $2 \times 100 =$　　　D. $8 \times 2 =$

E. $5 \times 20 =$　　　　F. $20 \times 2 =$

G. $4 \times 2 =$　　　　H. $6 \times 2 =$

I. $2 \times 7 =$　　　　J. $2 \times 0 =$

TIMS Bit

Ask students what strategies they use for solving these problems.

A.	18	B.	60
C.	200	D.	16
E.	100	F.	40
G.	8	H.	12
I.	14	J.	0

Right Angles 2

Find at least six right (square) angles in your classroom. Draw and label each object. Also, show where the right angle is on each.

TIMS Task

Some possible objects: the board, a book, a ruler, the teacher's desktop, a calendar, the top of a tissue box.

Chapter Books

1. Ann is reading a book that has about 400 pages. Each chapter in her book has about 25 pages. About how many chapters are there?

2. Marta's book has chapters that are about 15 pages long. Her book has 20 chapters. About how long is Marta's book?

TIMS Bit

1. 16 chapters. Students may count by 25s or repeatedly subtract 25 on the calculator. Relating 25 to 25¢ and 400 to $4 may be helpful for students trying to do the division in their heads.

2. 300 pages. Discuss strategies such as using a calculator or using the patterns in multiplying with multiples of 10.

 Tricky Change

Sally has a pocket of pennies, dimes, and quarters. She reaches in and pulls out four coins.

1. What amount of money might Sally have? List three different amounts.

2. What is the least she could have?

3. What is the most?

4. Could she have pulled out 12 cents? 8 cents? 25 cents? 46 cents?

TIMS Task

1. There are many possible answers. Three examples are: 40 cents (4 dimes), 52 cents (2 quarters and 2 pennies), 85 cents (3 quarters and 1 dime), 13 cents (1 dime and 3 pennies).

2. 4 pennies; 4 cents

3. 4 quarters; $1.00

4. No, No, No, Yes

Subtraction

Complete the following problems. Use pencil and paper or mental math to find the answers.

| 1. | 594 |
| | − 225 |

| 2. | 6784 |
| | − 2387 |

| 3. | 231 |
| | − 179 |

| 4. | 602 |
| | − 199 |

Explain your strategy for Question 3.

TIMS Bit

1. 369

2. 4397

3. 52

4. 403

Possible strategy: Count up 1 to 180, 20 to 200, 30 to 230, and 1 more to 231.

$1 + 20 + 30 + 1 = 52$

 Larry the Lizard Show

Use the Lizardland picture in the *Student Guide,* Unit 11, to solve the following problems. A total of 178 people attended the 10 A.M. show whereas 284 people attended the noon show.

1. How many more people attended the noon show than the 10 A.M. show?

2. How many people attended the first two shows?

3. How many empty seats were there during the first two shows?

TIMS Task

Students may use base-ten pieces or paper and pencil to find the answers.

1. 106 people

2. 462 people

3. $(300 + 300) − (178 + 284) = 138$ empty seats

| Student Questions | Teacher Notes |

 Bus Stop

Starting at 7:00 in the morning, a bus passes Ellen's stop every 15 minutes.

1. How many minutes must Ellen wait for the next bus if she gets to the stop at 9:05?

2. Will a bus come at 4:20 in the afternoon? How do you know?

TIMS Bit

You can work with a clock, showing the position of the minute hand as students count.

1. 10 minutes

2. No. 4:20 does not end in :00, :15, :30, or :45.

 Story Solving

1. $3 \times 9 = ?$ Write a story and draw a picture about 3×9. Write a number sentence on your picture.

2. $3 \times \frac{1}{2} = ?$ Write a story, and draw a picture about $3 \times \frac{1}{2}$. Write a number sentence on your picture.

TIMS Task

1. 27; Stories will vary.

2. $1\frac{1}{2}$; Students may wish to share their stories with the class. If there is a computer with a drawing program available, students may choose to draw their picture and tell their story on the computer.

K **Using Threes**

Do these problems in your head. Write only the answers.

A. $3 \times 5 =$ B. $7 \times 3 =$

C. $9 \times 3 =$ D. $3 \times 2 =$

E. $10 \times 3 =$ F. $3 \times 6 =$

G. $4 \times 3 =$ H. $3 \times 3 =$

I. $3 \times 1 =$ J. $8 \times 3 =$

Describe a strategy for 8×3.

TIMS Bit

Ask students what strategies they use for solving these problems.

A. 15   B. 21

C. 27   D. 6

E. 30   F. 18

G. 12   H. 9

I. 3   J. 24

Two possible strategies: skip count by 3s; $4 \times 3 = 12$, so 8×3 is double 12, or 24.

Dissection Puzzle 1

Trace and cut out the following triangles.

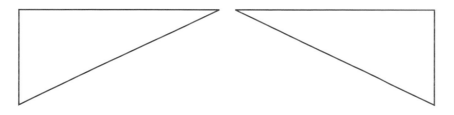

1. Put them edge to edge to make a rectangle.

2. Put them edge to edge to make a triangle.

3. Make four other shapes.

TIMS Task

You may wish to have students draw the shapes.

Ask students to describe all their shapes. How are they alike? How do they differ?

1.

2. or

3.

or

M **Quiz on 2s and 3s**

A. $4 \times 2 =$ B. $3 \times 2 =$

C. $5 \times 3 =$ D. $2 \times 10 =$

E. $6 \times 3 =$ F. $2 \times 5 =$

G. $10 \times 3 =$ H. $7 \times 2 =$

I. $8 \times 3 =$ J. $3 \times 3 =$

K. $8 \times 2 =$ L. $2 \times 2 =$

M. $9 \times 2 =$ N. $6 \times 2 =$

O. $3 \times 7 =$ P. $4 \times 3 =$

Q. $3 \times 9 =$ R. $3 \times 1 =$

TIMS Bit

This quiz is on the second group of multiplication facts, the 2s and 3s. We recommend 5 minutes for this quiz. You might want to allow students to change pens or pencils after the time is up and complete the remaining problems in a different color.

After students take the quiz, have them update their *Multiplication Facts I Know* charts.

Dissection Puzzle 2

1. Trace and cut out the shapes below.

2. Find all shapes that can be made by putting the three pieces edge to edge. Trace them on a piece of paper.

3. Make a data table that shows the area, perimeter, and lines of symmetry for each shape. Measure in square inches and inches.

TIMS Challenge

There are 5 noncongruent shapes.

A.

B.

C.

D.

E.

Discuss whether two shapes are the same. If you can turn or flip a shape and match another, the two shapes are the same. Some of the shapes can be made in more than one way. For example, shape D can be made as follows:

Shape	Perimeter (inches)	Number of lines of symmetry	Area (sq inches)
A	10	2	4
B	8	4	4
C	10	0	4
D	10	1	4
E	10	0	4

Lesson 1

Tangrams

Lesson Overview

Students attempt to cover a series of figures with all or some of the seven tangram pieces. Some figures are possible to cover; others are not. For those that cannot be covered, students explain why not. Then, students make their own tangram puzzles and share them with other students.

Key Content

- Representing shapes with tangrams, drawings, and words.
- Developing spatial visualization skills.
- Using geometric concepts (area and angle size) and skills to solve problems and communicate reasoning.

Key Vocabulary

- angle
- area
- edge
- tangram

Math Facts

DPP Bit A introduces the *Triangle Flash Cards: 2s* and *3s*. Bit C provides practice with the twos.

Homework

1. Assign Home Practice Part 1.
2. Have students share the puzzle they made on the *Making a Tangram Puzzle* Activity Page with a family member.
3. Assign some of the problems in the Puzzling Tangrams section of the *Tangrams* Activity Pages in the *Student Guide*.
4. Remind students to take home their *Triangle Flash Cards* to study with a family member.

Assessment

Use the Journal Prompt as an assessment.

Materials List

Supplies and Copies

Student	Teacher
Supplies for Each Student • set of tangram pieces • envelope for storing tangram pieces • envelope for storing flash cards • ruler	**Supplies**
Copies • 1 copy of *Tangram Pieces Master* per student pair, optional (*Unit Resource Guide* Page 32)	**Copies/Transparencies** • 1 transparency of *Hints for Puzzling Tangrams* (*Unit Resource Guide* Page 33)

All blackline masters including assessment, transparency, and DPP masters are also on the Teacher Resource CD.

Student Books

Tangrams (*Student Guide* Pages 158–165)
Triangle Flash Cards: 2s (*Discovery Assignment Book* Page 181)
Triangle Flash Cards: 3s (*Discovery Assignment Book* Page 183)
Making a Tangram Puzzle (*Discovery Assignment Book* Page 185)

Daily Practice and Problems and Home Practice

DPP items A–D (*Unit Resource Guide* Pages 14–15)
Home Practice Part 1 (*Discovery Assignment Book* Page 178)

Note: Classrooms whose pacing differs significantly from the suggested pacing of the units should use the Math Facts Calendar in Section 4 of the *Facts Resource Guide* to ensure students receive the complete math facts program.

A. Bit: Triangle Flash Cards: 2s and 3s
(URG p. 14)

With a partner, use your *Triangle Flash Cards* to quiz each other on the multiplication facts for the twos and threes. One partner covers the corner containing the highest number. This number will be the product. The second person multiplies the two uncovered numbers.

Separate the used cards into three piles: those facts you know and can answer quickly, those you can figure out with a strategy, and those you need to learn. Practice the last two piles again and then make a list of the facts you need to practice at home for homework.

Circle the facts you know and can answer quickly on your *Multiplication Facts I Know* chart.

B. Task: Right Angles 1 (URG p. 15)

1. How many right (square) angles do you see inside the shapes below? Circle them as you count.

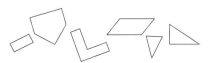

2. Tell how you decided which angles were right angles.

C. Bit: Using Twos (URG p. 15)

Do these problems in your head. Write only the answers.

A. $2 \times 9 =$	B. $3 \times 20 =$
C. $2 \times 100 =$	D. $8 \times 2 =$
E. $5 \times 20 =$	F. $20 \times 2 =$
G. $4 \times 2 =$	H. $6 \times 2 =$
I. $2 \times 7 =$	J. $2 \times 0 =$

D. Task: Right Angles 2 (URG p. 15)

Find at least six right (square) angles in your classroom. Draw and label each object. Also, show where the right angle is on each.

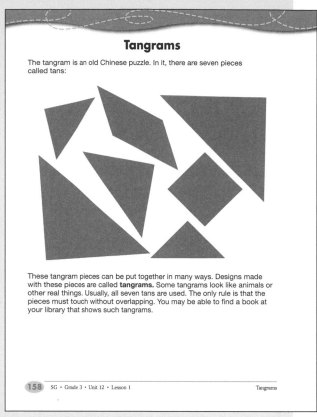

Tangrams

The tangram is an old Chinese puzzle. In it, there are seven pieces called tans:

These tangram pieces can be put together in many ways. Designs made with these pieces are called **tangrams.** Some tangrams look like animals or other real things. Usually, all seven tans are used. The only rule is that the pieces must touch without overlapping. You may be able to find a book at your library that shows such tangrams.

Student Guide - page 158

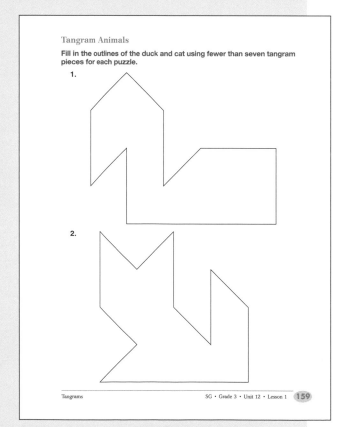

Tangram Animals

Fill in the outlines of the duck and cat using fewer than seven tangram pieces for each puzzle.

1.

2.

Student Guide - page 159 (Answers on p. 34)

Before the Activity

Each student needs one set of tangram pieces. Tangram pieces based on a 4-inch square are commercially available. If you do not wish to purchase the tangram pieces, you can make your own. Make copies of the *Tangram Pieces Master* on sturdy material like tagboard, card stock, or construction paper. We recommend that you or another adult cut apart the tangram pieces to assure accuracy.

TIMS Tip

If you purchase tangram pieces, the longest side of the largest triangle should be 4 inches long. However, many commercially available tangram pieces are a little smaller and will not fit exactly in the tangrams we have provided. You may want to reduce the tangram puzzles slightly on a copier or tell students that tangram pieces must fit inside the outline of the tangram rather than on the lines.

Teaching the Activity

Part 1 **Introducing Tangrams with Tangram Animals and More Tangram Animals**

One way to introduce tangrams is to read as a class the first *Tangrams* Activity Page in the *Student Guide.* This page introduces the seven tangram pieces and explains a general rule for making tangrams.

Another way to introduce tangrams is by reading *Grandfather Tang's Story* by Ann Tompert. In this book, a grandfather tells a fairy tale and illustrates it with tangrams.

Yet another way to begin is to make a tangram animal or other design on the overhead and then ask students to make and share their own tangrams. Provide a relatively unstructured time period for students to explore ways to use tangram pieces.

Explore dissections by using tangram pieces to cover the animal shapes on the Tangram Animals and More Tangram Animals sections of the *Student Guide.* Have students work individually or in pairs to solve the tangrams. In Tangram Animals, students use fewer than seven tangram pieces and in More Tangram Animals, students use all seven tangram pieces.

Content Note

Usually the word *tangram* refers to the puzzle and *tans* or *tangram pieces* refer to the seven pieces used to make the puzzle. However, the word *tangram* is frequently used to describe both the pieces and the puzzle.

Part 2 Puzzling Tangrams

In the Puzzling Tangrams section, students try to cover six shapes with the seven tangram pieces. Three of these shapes (shapes 5, 6, and 8) are possible. Shapes 7, 9, and 10 cannot be covered exactly with the seven tangram pieces. Have students work in pairs to solve each problem and compare solutions with another group.

Some students may give up after a short time. Encourage them to persist. Interesting problems require perseverance. If some students need a hint, suggest they try to place the large triangles first. Also, they may need to flip the parallelogram.

Question 5 asks students to make a square using all seven tangram pieces. Reassembling the seven tangram pieces into a square is difficult. On this activity page, an outline of the square and a background inch grid are provided to simplify the problem.

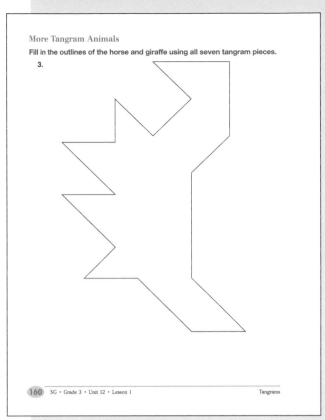

Student Guide - page 160 (Answers on p. 34)

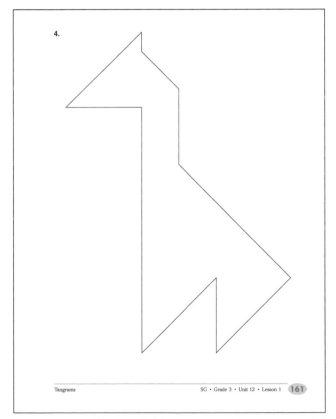

Student Guide - page 161 (Answers on p. 35)

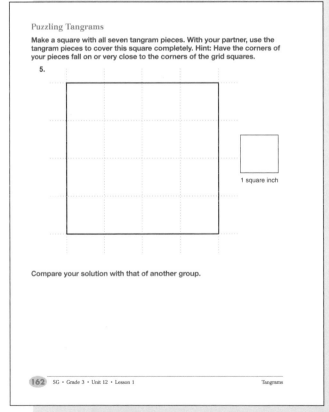

Student Guide - page 162 (Answers on p. 35)

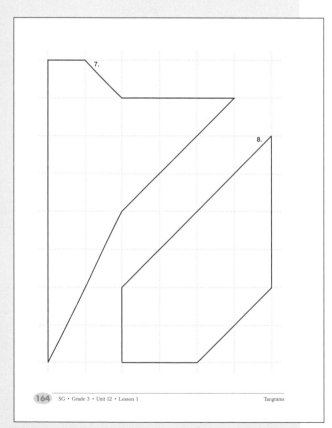

Student Guide - page 163 *(Answers on p. 36)*

Student Guide - page 164 *(Answers on p. 36)*

Some tangrams, such as the square, can be quite challenging. A number of strategies can be used for solving tangrams. The most obvious one is looking for angles that match. For example, if the shape has a square corner, look for one or more shapes that will make a square corner. A second strategy is to look at the lengths of the sides of the tangram pieces. There are four different lengths: 2 inches, 4 inches, about 1.41 inches, and about 2.83 inches. The square is 4 inches by 4 inches so the only way to get a 4-inch side is by using one 4-inch length or two 2-inch lengths. Since this observation makes the square puzzle much easier, we recommend not giving it until students have worked hard at their puzzles.

For *Question 5* if turns and flips are not counted as different, there is only one solution to the tangram square. If they are counted as different, then the eight solutions in Figure 3 are possible.

TIMS Tip

Note that the *Tangram Pieces Master* shows one way to make a square with the tangram pieces.

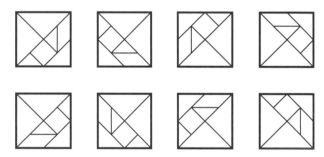

Figure 3: *Eight tangram squares*

To help students solve the puzzles in *Questions 5* and *6,* give them an additional hint by using the *Hints for Puzzling Tangrams* Transparency Master. This transparency gives the location of one of the tangram pieces for the first two puzzles.

If students have difficulty with *Question 9,* Figure 4 shows the location of one tangram piece or you may refer to the Answer Key for other hints.

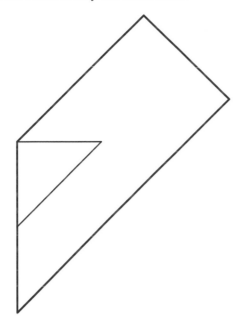

Figure 4: *Hint for Question 9*

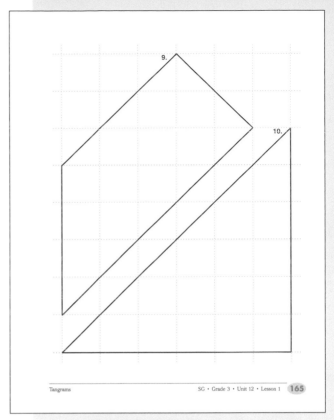

Student Guide - page 165 *(Answers on p. 37)*

In addition to geometric problem solving, the Puzzling Tangrams section raises three important issues: impossible problems, mathematical reasoning, and communication.

Students may not realize that every problem does not have a solution. Accordingly, they may waste time and effort attempting the impossible—such as, trying to cover shapes 7, 8, and 10 with the tangram pieces. We have provided some questions to guide students as they work on *Questions 6–10.* After reading and discussing the questions before *Question 6,* students should see that a tangram cannot be covered unless the area of the tangram is 16 square inches and the angles are the right size(s). By referring to the square in *Question 5,* students can see that the total area of the seven tangram pieces is 16 square inches.

Journal Prompt

Students can write a paragraph to convince a friend that it is impossible to cover shapes 7, 8, and 10 with the seven tangram pieces. Encourage the use of diagrams and mathematical concepts and terminology. Before the writing begins, you might brainstorm a list of words that may be useful.

There is a big difference between realizing that one cannot solve a problem and realizing that no one can ever solve the problem. The former realization is personal; the latter involves logical reasoning and mathematical arguments. To conclude, for example, that a shape's area precludes its ever being covered with the seven tangram pieces is a significant step on the road to higher level thinking.

Communication is vitally important in such problems. Mathematical arguments are tested and verified through a social process: The reasoning is made public and is accepted or rejected by a mathematical community. Accordingly, once students find a shape impossible to cover, they are to explain why in a way that persuades others. Using mathematical concepts and terminology can make explanations clearer and more convincing.

Part 3 Making a Tangram Puzzle

In this final section, students create their own tangrams on the *Making a Tangram Puzzle* Activity Page in the *Discovery Assignment Book*. They draw solutions for them on a separate sheet of paper. Remind students to use all seven tangram pieces and that pieces should not overlap. After creating their own tangrams, give students an opportunity to trade puzzles with their classmates.

TIMS Tip

Tracing around tangram pieces may be difficult because the pieces tend to slide as students move their pencils around them. It may be easier for students to place a dot at each corner of the tangram piece and connect the dots with a ruler.

Name _____ Date _____

Making a Tangram Puzzle

Make up your own tangram puzzle.
- Create a design using all seven tangram pieces.
- Make sure your pieces touch without overlapping.
- Then make an outline of your design in the space below.
- Trade tangrams with a friend. Try to solve each other's tangrams.

Tangrams   DAB • Grade 3 • Unit 12 • Lesson 1 **185**

Student Guide - page 185 *(Answers on p. 38)*

DPP Bit A introduces *Triangle Flash Cards* for the multiplication facts for the twos and threes. Bit C provides practice with the multiplication facts for the twos.

Homework and Practice

- DPP Tasks B and D review identifying right angles. This review will help with concepts in Lesson 2.

- After working on some of the shapes in *Questions 5–10* in class, students can finish the activity at home. To do this, they will need a set of tangram pieces (commercially bought or made using the *Tangram Pieces Master*). Stress that not every shape can be covered to avoid notes from frustrated parents about impossible homework.

- The *Making a Tangram Puzzle* Activity Page is also suitable for homework. Each student will need a set of tangram pieces. Encourage students to ask a family member to try to solve his or her puzzle.

- Students take home their *Triangle Flash Cards: 2s* and *3s* to study with a family member. The *Triangle Flash Cards: 2s* and *3s* can be found immediately following the Home Practice in the *Discovery Assignment Book*.

- Home Practice Part 1 provides practice with addition and subtraction computation.

Answers for Part 1 of the Home Practice are in the Answer Key at the end of this lesson and at the end of this unit.

Assessment

The Journal Prompt provides an opportunity to observe how students are using terminology and concepts to make explanations clear and convincing.

Extension

- **Convex Polygons.** Figure 5 shows the 13 convex polygons that can be made with the seven tangram pieces. Three of these appear in *Questions 5–10;* the other ten are also good puzzles. You can outline these on paper for students who are interested.

Name _____ Date _____

Unit 12 Home Practice

PART 1

Estimate to be sure your answers are reasonable.

1. 285
   +300

2. 285
   +318

3. 872
   −400

4. 872
   −490

5. Explain your estimation strategy for Question 4.

6. Marie has 748 marbles in her collection. She wants 1000. How many more marbles does she need?

PART 2

1. 115
   +27

2. 127
   +74

3. 280
   −33

4. 325
   −76

5. Explain a strategy for using mental math for Question 3.

6. Ted read a book for 43 minutes on Saturday and 29 minutes on Sunday.
   A. Did Ted read for more than one hour? Explain how you know.

   B. How many minutes did Ted read? _____

178 DAB • Grade 3 • Unit 12   DISSECTIONS

Student Guide - page 178 (Answers on p. 38)

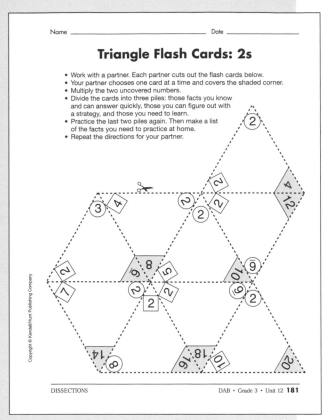

Discovery Assignment Book - page 181

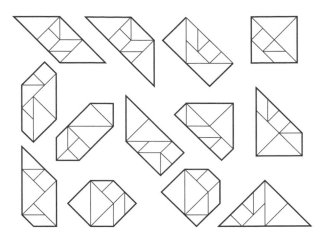

Figure 5: *Thirteen convex tangram polygons for use as extension puzzles*

- **Other Tangrams.** Provide an outline of a tangram to be covered or ask that a particular figure be made (e.g., a bird or a house). You can make up your own puzzles or find them in some of the books listed in Resources.

Literature Connection

- Tompert, Ann. *Grandfather Tang's Story.* Dragonfly Books, Cambridgeshire, UK, 1997.

Resources

- Crowley, Mary L. "The van Hiele Model of the Development of Geometric Thought." In Mary M. Lindquist (Ed.), *Learning and Teaching Geometry, K–12: 1987 Yearbook,* National Council of Teachers of Mathematics, Reston, VA.

- Gardner, Martin. *The 2nd Scientific American Book of Mathematical Puzzles and Diversions.* University of Chicago Press, Chicago, IL, 1987.

- Loyd, Sam, and Peter Van Note (Ed.). *The 8th Book of Tan: 700 Tangrams.* Dover Publications, New York, 1968.

- Read, Ronald C. *Tangrams—330 Puzzles.* Dover Publications, New York, 1980.

- Slocum, Jerry, and Jack Botermans. *Puzzles Old and New: How to Make and Solve Them.* University of Washington Press, Seattle, 1986.

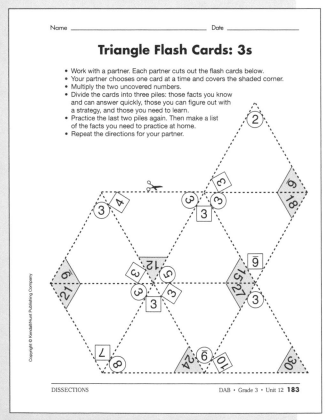

Discovery Assignment Book - page 183

Math Facts and Daily Practice and Problems

DPP Bit A introduces the *Triangle Flash Cards: 2s* and *3s*. Bit C provides practice with the twos. Tasks B and D review identifying right angles.

Part 1. Introducing Tangrams with Tangram Animals and More Tangram Animals

1. Introduce tangrams by reading the first *Tangrams* Activity Page as a class, reading *Grandfather Tang's Story*, or making a tangram on the overhead. Ask students to make and share their own tangrams.

2. Students find ways to cover the tangrams in the Tangram Animals and More Tangram Animals sections. *(Questions 1–4)*

Part 2. Puzzling Tangrams

1. Student pairs find and share solutions for the tangram square for *Question 5*.

2. Students read and discuss the questions that precede *Question 6*.

3. Students solve *Questions 6–10* and explain why some shapes are impossible to cover.

Part 3. Making a Tangram Puzzle

Students create their own tangrams and share them with classmates on the *Making a Tangram Puzzle* Activity Page in the *Discovery Assignment Book*.

Homework

1. Assign Home Practice Part 1.

2. Have students share the puzzle they made on the *Making a Tangram Puzzle* Activity Page with a family member.

3. Assign some of the problems in the Puzzling Tangrams section of the *Tangrams* Activity Pages in the *Student Guide*.

4. Remind students to take home their *Triangle Flash Cards* to study with a family member.

Assessment

Use the Journal Prompt as an assessment

Extension

1. Challenge students to solve polygon tangram puzzles.

2. Make other tangram puzzles for students to solve or challenge students to create a tangram puzzle that resembles a certain shape (e.g., a bird or a house).

Connection

Read and discuss *Grandfather Tang's Story* by Ann Tompert.

Answer Key is on pages 34–38.

Notes:

Tangram Pieces Master

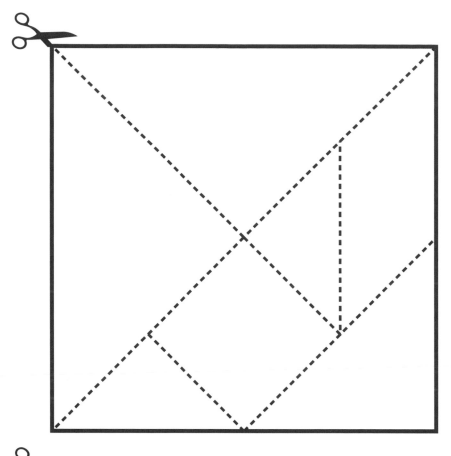

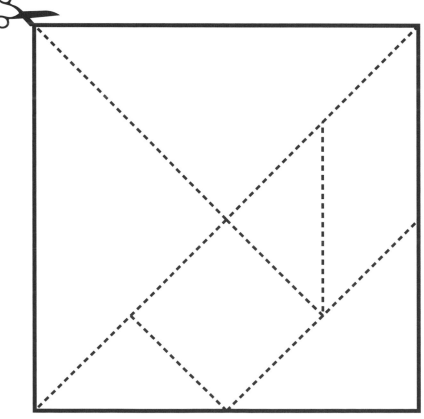

Blackline Master

Hints for Puzzling Tangrams

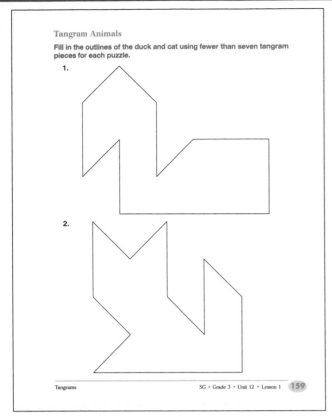

Tangram Animals

Fill in the outlines of the duck and cat using fewer than seven tangram pieces for each puzzle.

1.

2.

Tangrams   SG • Grade 3 • Unit 12 • Lesson 1   159

Student Guide - page 159

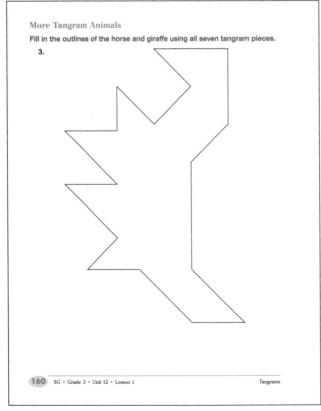

More Tangram Animals

Fill in the outlines of the horse and giraffe using all seven tangram pieces.

3.

160   SG • Grade 3 • Unit 12 • Lesson 1   Tangrams

Student Guide - page 160

Student Guide (p. 159)

1.

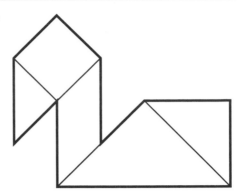

2.

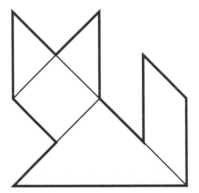

Student Guide (p. 160)

3.

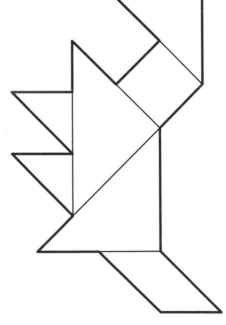

Student Guide (p. 161)

4.

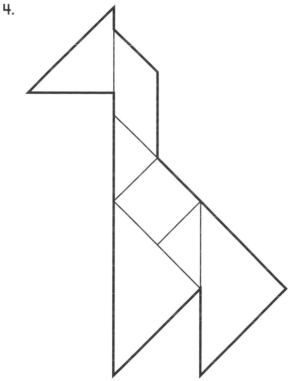

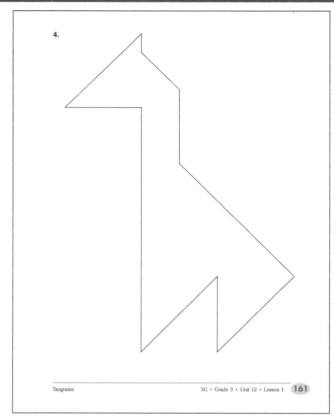

Student Guide - page 161

Student Guide (p. 162)

5.

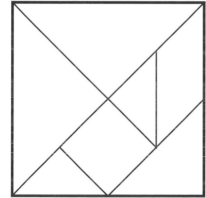

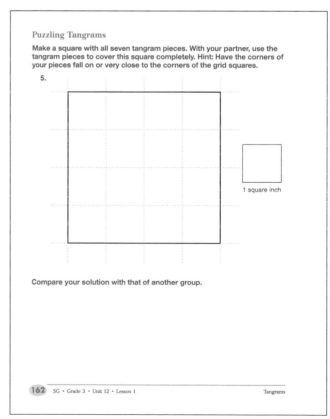

Student Guide - page 162

Try to use all seven pieces to cover each shape in Questions 6–10. Some of the shapes can be covered with the pieces, and some cannot. If you cannot cover a shape exactly using all the pieces, explain why. As you try to solve the puzzles, use the questions below to help.

    A. What is the area of the square in Question 5? This is the total area of all your tangram pieces.

    B. What is the area of the shape you are trying to cover?

    C. Can you find a tangram piece to fit in each corner of the shape?

    D. Will you be able to use all the pieces to cover the shape?

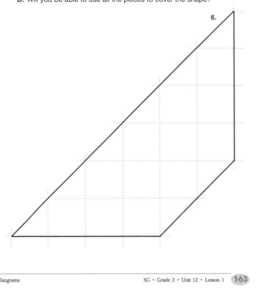

Tangrams   SG • Grade 3 • Unit 12 • Lesson 1   163

Student Guide - page 163

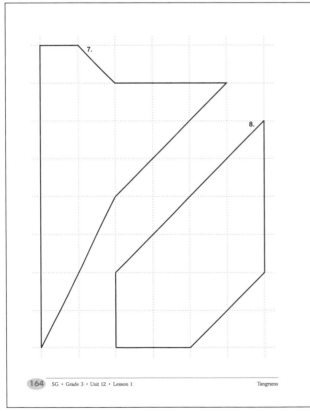

164   SG • Grade 3 • Unit 12 • Lesson 1   Tangrams

Student Guide - page 164

Student Guide (p. 163)

5. **A.** The area of the square in **Question 5** is 16 sq in.

    B. The area of each of the three shapes in **Question 5, 6, 7,** and **9** is 16 sq in. The shape in **Question 8** is 14 sq in. The shape in **Question 10** is 18 sq in.

    C. The angle at the bottom of the shape in **Question 7** cannot be matched with any tangram piece.

    D. The shapes in **Questions 7, 8,** and **10** cannot be covered with all the pieces.

6. Answers may vary. One possible solution is shown below.

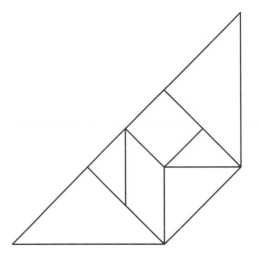

Student Guide (p. 164)

7. This puzzle is impossible. The bottom angle in this shape cannot be matched with any of the tangram pieces.

8. This shape cannot be filled using the 7 tangram pieces because the area of this shape is only 14 sq inches. The total area of the tangram pieces is 16 sq in. The shape can be covered with exactly 6 pieces. Which tan must be left out?

Student Guide (p. 165)

9. Answers may vary. Two possible solutions
   are shown.

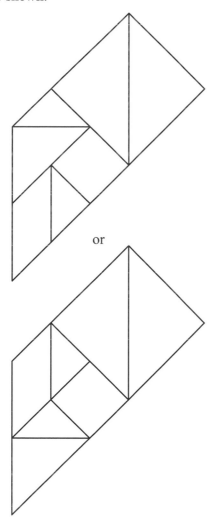

or

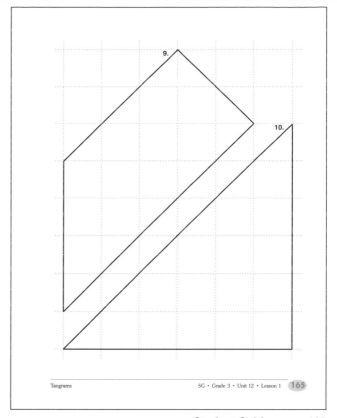

Student Guide - page 165

10. The area of this triangle is 18 sq in. It is too
    large to be covered by only the seven tangram
    pieces.

Discovery Assignment Book (p. 178)

Home Practice*

Part 1

1. 585

2. 603

3. 472

4. 382

5. Possible answer: 872 is close to 900 and 490 is close to 500. So the answer is close to $900 - 500 = 400$.

6. 252 marbles

Name _____ Date _____

Unit 12 Home Practice

PART 1

Estimate to be sure your answers are reasonable.

1. 285 +300   2. 285 +318   3. 872 −400   4. 872 −490

5. Explain your estimation strategy for Question 4.

6. Marie has 748 marbles in her collection. She wants 1000. How many more marbles does she need?

PART 2

1. 115 +27   2. 127 +74   3. 280 −33   4. 325 −76

5. Explain a strategy for using mental math for Question 3.

6. Ted read a book for 43 minutes on Saturday and 29 minutes on Sunday.
   A. Did Ted read for more than one hour? Explain how you know.

   B. How many minutes did Ted read? _____

178 DAB • Grade 3 • Unit 12   DISSECTIONS

Discovery Assignment Book - page 178

Discovery Assignment Book (p. 185)

Making a Tangram Puzzle

Answers will vary.

Name _____ Date _____

Making a Tangram Puzzle

Make up your own tangram puzzle.
- Create a design using all seven tangram pieces.
- Make sure your pieces touch without overlapping.
- Then make an outline of your design in the space below.
- Trade tangrams with a friend. Try to solve each other's tangrams.

Tangrams   DAB • Grade 3 • Unit 12 • Lesson 1 **185**

Discovery Assignment Book - page 185

*Answers for all the Home Practice in the *Discovery Assignment Book* are at the end of the unit.

Lesson 2

Building with Triangles

Lesson Overview

Estimated Class Sessions

1-2

Students make shapes by putting two or three isosceles right triangles together edge to edge. The shapes are recorded, measured, described, and analyzed. In Lesson 3 *Building with Four Triangles,* the work is extended to four triangles.

Key Content

- Representing shapes using manipulatives, drawings, and words.
- Using flips and turns to identify shapes that are congruent.
- Analyzing and classifying shapes using their properties (number of sides, corners, right angles, and lines of symmetry).
- Measuring area and perimeter.
- Solving geometric problems and explaining the reasoning.

Key Vocabulary

- congruent
- corner (vertex)
- line symmetry
- line of symmetry
- square corner (right angle)

Homework

1. Assign the Building with Three Triangles section for homework.
2. Assign Home Practice Part 2.

Assessment

1. During the activity observe students' abilities to identify right angles, recognize congruent shapes, show lines of symmetry, and measure area and perimeter. Record your observations on the *Observational Assessment Record.*
2. Use the Journal Prompt to assess students' abilities to explain their reasoning.

Curriculum Sequence

Before This Unit

Line Symmetry

Students identified line symmetry in Grade 2 Unit 15.

Area and Perimeter

Students measured area in Grade 3 Unit 5. They measured perimeters of regular shapes in Unit 7 Lesson 6 *Walking around Shapes*.

After This Unit

Line Symmetry

Students will explore symmetry further in Grade 4 Unit 9.

Area and Perimeter

Students will measure area and perimeter in Grade 4 Unit 2.

Analyzing and Describing Shapes

Students will analyze and describe three-dimensional shapes in Grade 3 Unit 18.

Materials List

Supplies and Copies

Student	Teacher
Supplies for Each Student • scissors • centimeter ruler • markers or crayons **Supplies for Each Student Group** • envelope for storing triangles • 3 small triangles from 2 tangram sets • square from a set of tangrams, optional	**Supplies**
Copies • 1 copy of *Lines of Symmetry* per student, optional (*Unit Resource Guide* Page 51)	**Copies/Transparencies** • 1 or 2 copies of *Right Triangle Master* on heavy paper, optional (*Unit Resource Guide* Page 52) • 1 transparency of *When Are Shapes the Same?* (*Unit Resource Guide* Page 53) • 1 copy of *Observational Assessment Record* to be used throughout this unit (*Unit Resource Guide* Page 11–12)

All blackline masters including assessment, transparency, and DPP masters are also on the Teacher Resource CD.

Student Books
Building with Triangles (*Student Guide* Pages 166–169)
Building with Triangles Data Table 1 (*Discovery Assignment Book* Page 187)
Building with Triangles Data Table 2 (*Discovery Assignment Book* Page 188)

Daily Practice and Problems and Home Practice
DPP items E–F (*Unit Resource Guide* Page 16)
Home Practice Part 2 (*Discovery Assignment Book* Page 178)

Note: Classrooms whose pacing differs significantly from the suggested pacing of the units should use the Math Facts Calendar in Section 4 of the *Facts Resource Guide* to ensure students receive the complete math facts program.

Assessment Tools
Observational Assessment Record (*Unit Resource Guide* Pages 11–12)

Suggestions for using the DPPs are on page 49.

E. Bit: Chapter Books (URG p. 16)

1. Ann is reading a book that has about 400 pages. Each chapter in her book has about 25 pages. About how many chapters are there?

2. Marta's book has chapters that are about 15 pages long. Her book has 20 chapters. About how long is Marta's book?

F. Task: Tricky Change
(URG p. 16)

Sally has a pocket of pennies, dimes, and quarters. She reaches in and pulls out four coins.

1. What amount of money might Sally have? List three different amounts.
2. What is the least she could have?
3. What is the most?
4. Could she have pulled out 12 cents? 8 cents? 25 cents? 46 cents?

For this lesson, each student pair needs three isosceles right triangles with a two-inch hypotenuse as shown in Figure 6. The smallest triangles in a set of tangrams are this size. If tangrams of this size are not available, a copy of the *Right Triangle Master* Blackline Master will provide enough triangles for eight pairs of students. Since these triangles will be used for several days, the copies should be made of a sturdy material like card stock, tag board, or construction paper and students should store their triangles in envelopes.

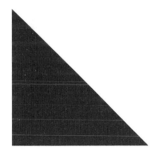

Figure 6: *Student groups need three triangles of this size and shape to complete this lesson.*

As part of this lesson, students draw lines of symmetry on the shapes they build. Second-grade students using *Math Trailblazers* learned to identify shapes with line symmetry. If you have students who are new to *Math Trailblazers* who have not studied line symmetry before, use the *Lines of Symmetry* Blackline Master to prepare them for this lesson or have a class discussion about lines of symmetry.

A shape has **line symmetry** if after flipping the shape along that line, it still looks the same. You can show that a shape has line symmetry by folding the shape into two matching halves. (The halves must fold perfectly onto each other.) The fold line is called the **line of symmetry.** Students should cut out the shapes on the *Lines of Symmetry* Blackline Master and try to fold each shape into matching halves. Remind them that the fold line is called the line of symmetry and ask them to draw the lines of symmetry on the appropriate shapes. Note that a shape can have more than one line of symmetry. Students draw all the lines of symmetry they find on a shape. Figure 7 shows the lines of symmetry for shapes A and C on the *Lines of Symmetry* Blackline Master. Shape B does not have line symmetry.

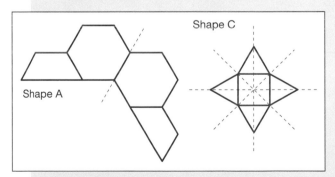

Figure 7: *Lines of symmetry*

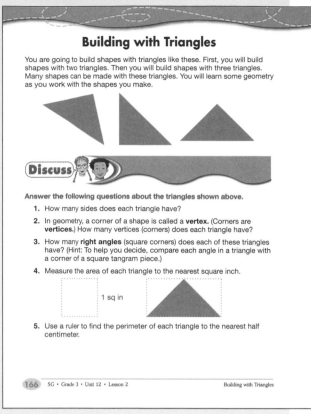

Building with Triangles

You are going to build shapes with triangles like these. First, you will build shapes with two triangles. Then you will build shapes with three triangles. Many shapes can be made with these triangles. You will learn some geometry as you work with the shapes you make.

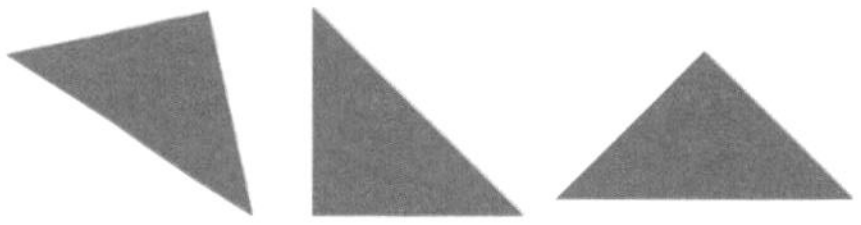

Discuss

Answer the following questions about the triangles shown above.

1. How many sides does each triangle have?
2. In geometry, a corner of a shape is called a **vertex.** (Corners are **vertices.**) How many vertices (corners) does each triangle have?
3. How many **right angles** (square corners) does each of these triangles have? (Hint: To help you decide, compare each angle in a triangle with a corner of a square tangram piece.)
4. Measure the area of each triangle to the nearest square inch.

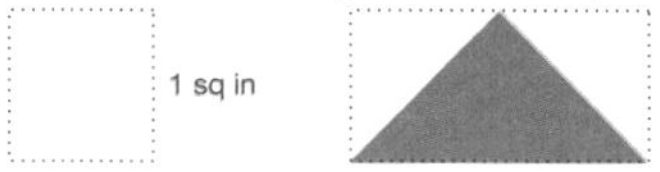
1 sq in

5. Use a ruler to find the perimeter of each triangle to the nearest half centimeter.

166 SG • Grade 3 • Unit 12 • Lesson 2 Building with Triangles

***Student Guide* - page 166** *(Answers on p. 54)*

There is one rule for building shapes with these triangles. The triangles must be put together edge to edge, like this:

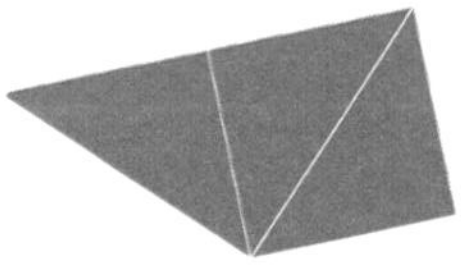

not like this.

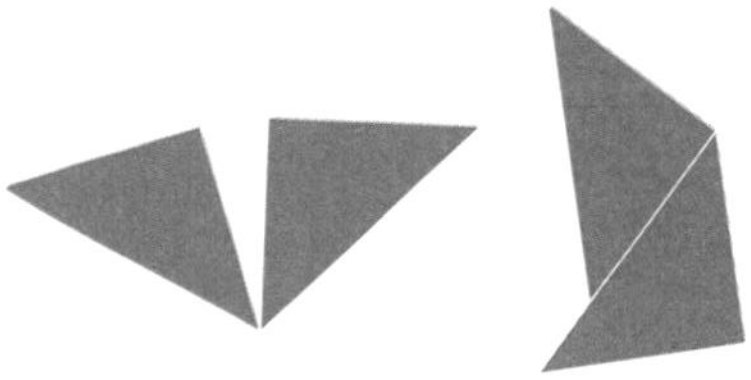

We need this rule; otherwise, there are too many shapes that can be made.

Building with Two Triangles

To start, you will need two triangles that are the same shape and size as these. You can use triangles from a set of tangrams.

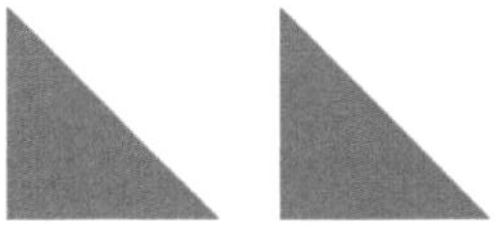

You will also need a ruler, paper and pencil, a marker or crayon, and a data table.

Building with Triangles SG • Grade 3 • Unit 12 • Lesson 2 167

***Student Guide* - page 167**

Teaching the Activity

This activity develops many of the unit's key ideas—working with shapes, discussing their properties, and measuring area and perimeter. These lessons are suitable for students working in pairs if each pair has three triangles.

Part 1 Building with Triangles

Students discuss the properties, area, and perimeter of one triangle. The discussion questions on the *Building with Triangles* Activity Pages in the *Student Guide* introduce or review concepts and vocabulary used in the lesson. For example, ***Question 2*** defines a **vertex** as a corner of a shape. ***Question 3*** asks students to identify any right angles in the triangle by comparing each angle to a corner of a square. (If square tangram pieces are not available, students can use a corner of a piece of paper.) ***Questions 4*** and ***5*** ask students to measure the area of a triangle to the nearest square inch and the perimeter to the nearest half centimeter. From the drawing, students can see that each triangle measures one square inch and use a ruler to measure the perimeter.

These pages also introduce the edge-to-edge rule that is used throughout the rest of the unit. By this, we mean that shapes must be built with only edges of the same length touching and with those edges meeting along their entire length. Shapes with triangles that overlap or touch only at one point are not used in this activity. This rule limits the number of figures that can be made and facilitates record keeping.

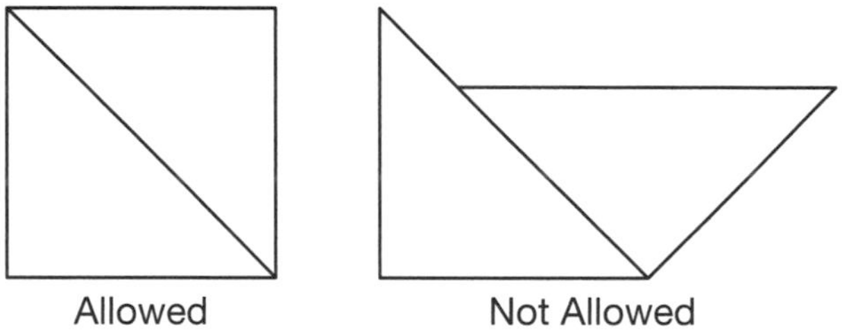
Allowed
Not Allowed

Figure 8: *Edge-to-edge rule*

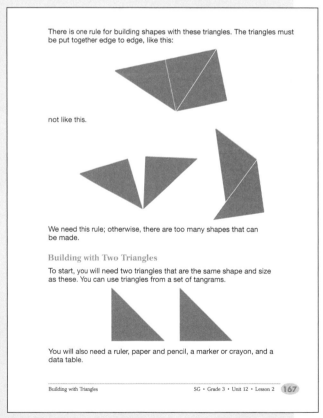

Part 2 Building with Two Triangles

In this section, students make all possible shapes using two of their triangles. They keep a record of their shapes and analyze them. Figure 9 shows the only three shapes that can be made and names students have given them.

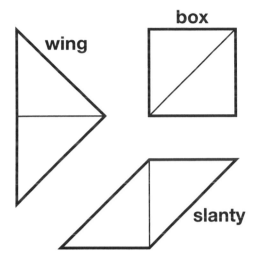

Figure 9: *Shapes made with two isosceles right triangles*

The *Building with Triangles* Activity Pages also state a second rule: Turns and flips of a given shape (congruent figures) are considered to be the same shape. You might also discuss the fact that we could consider turns and flips to be different if we wished—in some contexts, turned and flipped shapes may not be equivalent.

You can use the *When Are Shapes the Same?* Transparency Master to demonstrate turns, flips, and congruence. Place the transparency on the overhead projector and ask students if the two shapes are congruent. Remind them that the shapes are **congruent** if you can turn or flip one so it exactly covers the other. Encourage students to make copies of shapes to help them decide congruence. After some discussion, cut the transparency along the dotted line and show students that the lower figure can be turned and flipped to exactly cover the upper figure. Use other figures as needed to explore congruence. Take two sheets of acetate to make two copies of a shape. One copy can be turned or flipped to check congruence.

Student Guide - page 168 (Answers on p. 54)

Content Note

Two Parallelograms? Students are likely to make the following parallelograms.

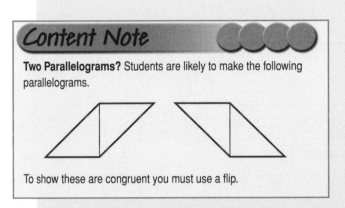

To show these are congruent you must use a flip.

Same and Different: Flips, Turns, and Congruence. The three shapes in Figure 9 are all that can be made if turns and flips are not counted as different. This rule follows common mathematical convention: Shapes that are congruent are usually understood to be "the same." This rule also conveniently limits the number of different shapes that are possible, but it may also confuse some students. Although the shape in Figure 10 is a square, many students would say that it is a diamond and not a square because it is turned from the standard position.

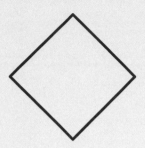

Figure 10: *Is this figure a square?*

As students find shapes they can make with two triangles, you might ask them to draw them on the board. This will provide good material for a discussion of same and different. You will probably find that these board drawings are not particularly accurate—angles, in particular, are likely to be distorted. Their drawings can motivate a discussion of the relative sizes of the parts of triangles. We do not recommend that you refer to the triangles as "isosceles right triangles with a 2-inch hypotenuse," but you will want students to notice that two angles are equal, that the other angle is a right angle (square corner), that two sides are equal, and that the third side is longer.

Naming the shapes will make talking about them easier. Ask students to propose names as they draw the shapes on the board. Standard mathematical terminology is not necessary, since the concept of a mathematical definition is better dealt with in later grades. For example, calling the shapes in Figure 9 triangle, square, and parallelogram may reinforce the incorrect notion that a square is not a parallelogram. Calling the shapes "wing," "box," and "slanty," for example, avoids this danger. These issues are explored further in the Professor Peabody's Shape Riddles section of Lesson 3 *Building with Four Triangles.*

After students have found their shapes, *Questions 6* and *7* tell them to record each shape on paper and to outline the outside border using a marker or crayon. This will facilitate counting the sides and corners. Next, students analyze their shapes. *Question 8* gives directions for recording information about each shape on the *Building with Triangles Data Table 1* Activity Page in the *Discovery Assignment Book.*

Name _____ Date _____

Building with Triangles
Data Table 1

Number of triangles used _____ Partner(s) _____

Name of Shape	Sketch	No. of Sides	No. of Corners (vertices)	No. of Right Angles	Area (sq in)	Perimeter (cm)

Building with Triangles   DAB • Grade 3 • Unit 12 • Lesson 2 **187**

Discovery Assignment Book **- page 187**

Journal Prompt

Ask students to write how they know they have found all shapes possible with two triangles put together edge to edge. You might tell them that "Mr. I.B. Dense" thinks he has a different shape from those in Figure 9. Ask them to write a letter to him explaining why he must be wrong.

Counting sides and corners *(Questions 8C and 8D)* is not too difficult although some students may be distracted by the interior triangles. They may, for example, claim that the shape on the left in Figure 11 has four sides. In a sense, this is correct, but this is not the sense we mean. Only the outline is to be considered. Drawings like the one on the right in Figure 11 may be easier to analyze.

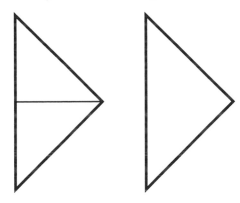

Figure 11: *A shape with interior triangles shown and not shown*

Counting right angles is tricky *(Question 8E).* Most students have difficulty understanding what a right angle is. Even if they do, right angles can be hard to pick out among the visual clutter of the interior triangles. Using the corner of a square or a piece of paper or a book (as in *Question 3*) is one way to check if an angle is right or not. Using outline shapes (with interior triangles not showing as in Figure 11) may also help. Items B and D in the Daily Practice and Problems familiarize students with right angles and should be completed before students try to count right angles in their shapes.

Questions 8F and *8G* ask students to record the area and perimeter of each shape. Note that finding the area should be straightforward since each triangle measures approximately one square inch. Students need only count the number of triangles in each figure. Students may need to review perimeter, a concept that was introduced in *Walking around Shapes* in Unit 7 *Multiplication and Division.* One way to find the perimeter is to measure the length of each side with a ruler and then to add those lengths; another way is to begin measuring each side at the spot on the ruler where the previous side ended. Inches or centimeters can be used to measure— either way, the answers will not come out even. However, since centimeters are smaller (hence, more accurate) and also yield fractions that are more manageable, we recommend that students measure the perimeter to the nearest half centimeter.

F. Find the area of each shape. (Hint: The area of each small triangle is 1 square inch.)

G. Use a ruler to measure the perimeter of each shape to the nearest half centimeter.

Name of Shape	Sketch	No. of Sides	No. of Corners (vertices)	No. of Right Angles	Area (sq in)	Perimeter (cm)
wing		3	3	1	2	17

9. **A.** Which of your shapes have line symmetry? (If a shape has **line symmetry**, you can fold the shape in half and the halves will match exactly.)

    B. Draw lines of symmetry on your sketches in the second column of your data table. Follow the example.

10. Find and describe at least one pattern in your table.

Building with Three Triangles

11. Now, find all the shapes that can be made by putting three triangles together edge to edge. Use three triangles like these.

Analyze each of the shapes using Questions 8 and 9 as a guide. Write your answers in a table like the one you used in your work with two triangles.

12. Find and describe a pattern in your new table.

Building with Triangles   SG • Grade 3 • Unit 12 • Lesson 2   169

Student Guide - page 169 (Answers on p. 55)

TIMS Tip

To help students recall what perimeter is, you might introduce a bug named Perry Meter. Perry walks completely around the outside of a plane figure and when he reaches his starting point, he reports the distance he has traveled. For convenience, Perry should start at a corner, but this is not strictly necessary.

A relationship exists between the number of sides and the number of corners of these shapes: They are equal. This is one of the patterns we expect students to find when they have completed their data tables *(Question 10).*

Part 3 **Building with Three Triangles**

Question 11 asks students to repeat the basic steps in *Questions 6–10* using three triangles in their data collection. Figure 12 shows the four shapes that can be made with three triangles and names students have given them. If your students did well with the two-triangle case, consider using the Building with Three Triangles section as homework.

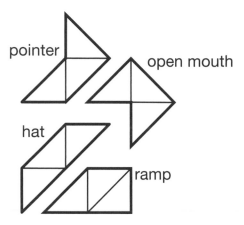

Figure 12: *Shapes from three isosceles right triangles put together edge to edge*

The three-triangle case is not much different from the two-triangle case. One new wrinkle is that one of the shapes can be dissected in two different ways. Figure 13 shows the shape and both dissections. For simplicity, consider these shapes to be the same, just as we consider flips and turns to be the same. Your students may not raise this point, and we recommend not bringing it up if it is not mentioned. The important thing to stress is different outline shapes; the interior triangles do not matter.

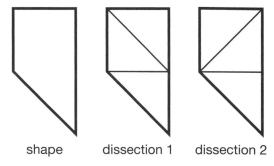

shape   dissection 1   dissection 2

Figure 13: *Alternate dissections of a shape*

Homework and Practice

- DPP Bit E provides two word problems using multiplication. DPP Task F is a word problem involving money.

- The section Building with Three Triangles is appropriate for homework after students have completed Building with Two Triangles. Note that students will need triangles, rulers, and the *Building with Triangles Data Table 2* in the *Discovery Assignment Book*.

- Home Practice Part 2 provides further practice with addition and subtraction computation.

Answers for Part 2 of the Home Practice are in the Answer Key at the end of this lesson and at the end of this unit.

Assessment

- Assess students' abilities to identify right angles, to recognize if two shapes are congruent, to show line symmetry, and to measure area and perimeter. Record your observations on the *Observational Assessment Record*.

- Use the Journal Prompt to observe how students are using terminology and concepts to explain their reasoning.

Name _____ Date _____

Building with Triangles
Data Table 2

Number of triangles used _____ Partner(s) _____

Name of Shape	Sketch	No. of Sides	No. of Corners (vertices)	No. of Right Angles	Area (sq in)	Perimeter (cm)

188 DAB · Grade 3 · Unit 12 · Lesson 2   Building with Triangles

Discovery Assignment Book - page 188

Name _____ Date _____

Unit 12 Home Practice

PART 1

Estimate to be sure your answers are reasonable.

1. 285
   +300

2. 285
   +318

3. 872
   −400

4. 872
   −490

5. Explain your estimation strategy for Question 4.

6. Marie has 748 marbles in her collection. She wants 1000. How many more marbles does she need?

PART 2

1. 115
   +27

2. 127
   +74

3. 280
   −33

4. 325
   −76

5. Explain a strategy for using mental math for Question 3.

6. Ted read a book for 43 minutes on Saturday and 29 minutes on Sunday.
   A. Did Ted read for more than one hour? Explain how you know.

   B. How many minutes did Ted read? _____

178 DAB · Grade 3 · Unit 12   DISSECTIONS

Discovery Assignment Book - page 178 (Answers on p. 56)

URG · Grade 3 · Unit 12 · Lesson 2   **49**

At a Glance

Math Facts and Daily Practice and Problems

DPP items E and F are word problems.

Part 1. Building with Triangles

1. Students answer *Questions 1–5* in the *Student Guide* that introduce and review vocabulary students will use to analyze shapes.
2. Introduce the edge-to-edge rule.

Part 2. Building with Two Triangles

1. Use the *When Are Shapes the Same?* Transparency Master to define congruent shapes and discuss "same" and "different."
2. Students make shapes using two triangles, draw them on paper, and outline the outside border in markers or crayons. *(Questions 6–7)*
3. Students analyze the shapes using *Question 8* and record their findings on the *Building with Triangles Data Table 1* Activity Page in the *Discovery Assignment Book.*
4. Students identify those shapes with line symmetry and draw the lines of symmetry on the sketches of the shapes in their data tables. *(Question 9)*
5. For *Question 10,* students describe patterns they find in their data tables.

Part 3. Building with Three Triangles

For *Questions 11–12,* students build shapes with three triangles, analyze the shapes, and record their findings on the *Building with Triangles Data Table 2.*

Homework

1. Assign the Building with Three Triangles section for homework.
2. Assign Home Practice Part 2.

Assessment

1. During the activity observe students' abilities to identify right angles, recognize congruent shapes, show lines of symmetry, and measure area and perimeter. Record your observations on the *Observational Assessment Record.*
2. Use the Journal Prompt to assess students' abilities to explain their reasoning.

Answer Key is on pages 54–56.

Notes:

Lines of Symmetry

1. Cut out the shapes.

2. Fold the shapes to see if they have a line of symmetry.

3. Draw the lines of symmetry on each shape.

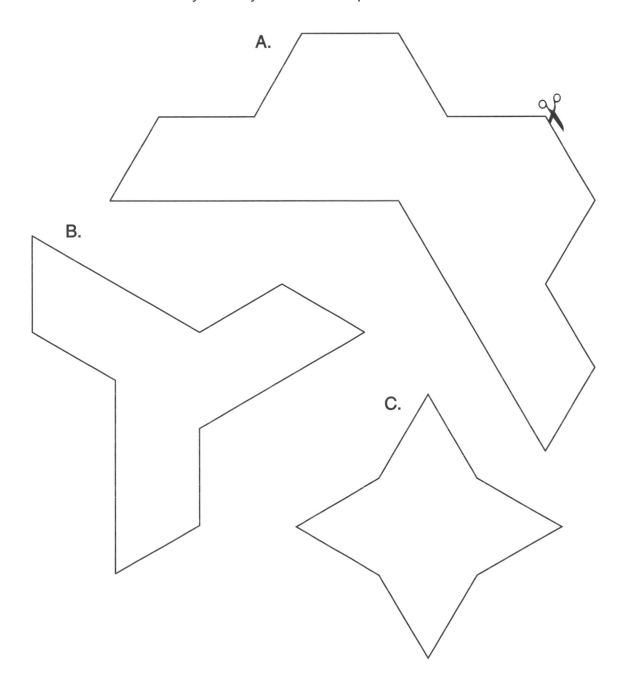

Right Triangle Master

When Are Shapes the Same?

Are these two figures congruent?

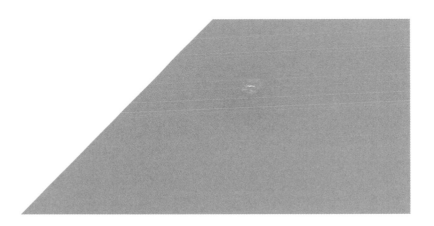

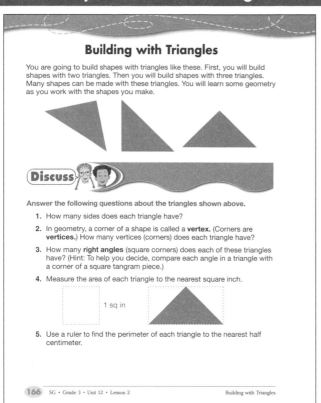

Student Guide - page 166

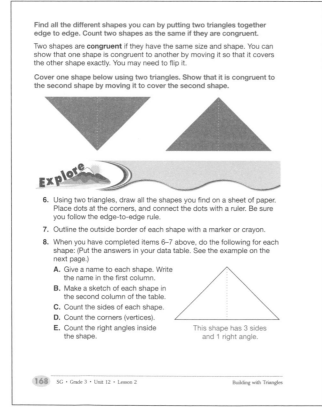

Student Guide - page 168

Student Guide (p. 166)

1. 3 sides

2. 3 corners or vertices

3. 1 square corner or right angle

4. 1 sq in

5. 12 cm

Student Guide (p. 168)

6.–8. A. Names for these shapes will vary.

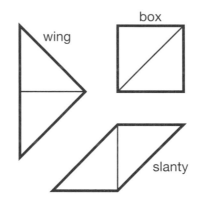

8. A.–G.

Name	# Sides	# Corners	# right angle	Area (sq in)	Perimeter (cm)
wing	3	3	1	2 sq in	17 cm
box	4	4	4	2 sq in	14 cm
slanty	4	4	0	2 sq in	17 cm

Student Guide (p. 169)

9. A. wing and box
   B.

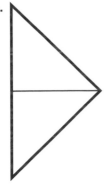

10. Answers will vary. The area of all three shapes is 2 sq in. The perimeter of two of the types is the same—17 cm. The perimeters of wing and slanty are made up of the same sides—2 short sides (the legs of the right triangles) and 2 long sides (the hypotenuse). The number of sides always equals the number of corners.

11. The names of the shapes will vary. Note: Only the interior angles were counted for 90° angles. Your students may choose to count both.

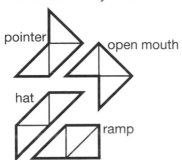

Name	# Sides	# Corners	# right angle	Area (sq in)	Perimeter (cm)
pointer	5	5	1	3 sq in	22 cm
open mouth	5	5	2	3 sq in	22 cm
hat	4	4	0	3 sq in	22 cm
ramp	4	4	2	3 sq in	19 cm

F. Find the area of each shape. (Hint: The area of each small triangle is 1 square inch.)
G. Use a ruler to measure the perimeter of each shape to the nearest half centimeter.

Name of Shape	Sketch	No. of Sides	No. of Corners (vertices)	No. of Right Angles	Area (sq in)	Perimeter (cm)
wing		3	3	1	2	17

9. A. Which of your shapes have line symmetry? (If a shape has **line symmetry,** you can fold the shape in half and the halves will match exactly.)
   B. Draw lines of symmetry on your sketches in the second column of your data table. Follow the example.
10. Find and describe at least one pattern in your table.

Building with Three Triangles

11. Now, find all the shapes that can be made by putting three triangles together edge to edge. Use three triangles like these.

Analyze each of the shapes using Questions 8 and 9 as a guide. Write your answers in a table like the one you used in your work with two triangles.

12. Find and describe a pattern in your new table.

Student Guide - page 169

12. Answers will vary. The number of corners equals the number of sides. The area of all four shapes is the same—3 sq in. The perimeter of three of the shapes is the same—22 cm.

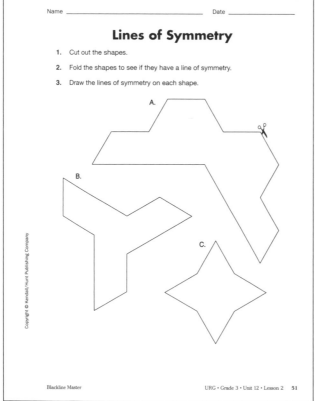

Discovery Assignment Book - page 178

Discovery Assignment Book (p. 178)

Home Practice*

Part 2

  1. 142

  2. 201

  3. 247

  4. 249

  5. Possible strategy: $280 - 30 = 250$ and $250 - 3 = 247$.

  6. A. Yes; $40 + 20 = 60$; 43 and 29 are greater than 40 and 20

     B. 72 minutes or 1 hour and 12 minutes

Unit Resource Guide (p. 51)

Lines of Symmetry

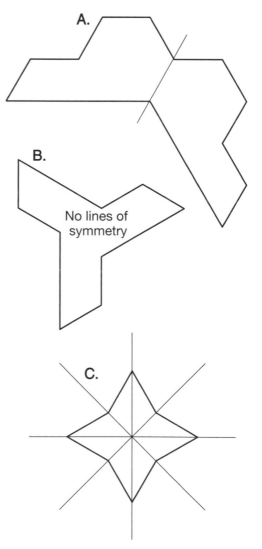

Unit Resource Guide - page 51

*Answers for all the Home Practice in the *Discovery Assignment Book* are at the end of the unit.

Building with Four Triangles

Lesson Overview

Estimated Class Sessions

2

This activity continues and extends the previous activity, *Building with Triangles.* Students investigate shapes that can be made with four isosceles right triangles put together edge to edge.

Key Content

- Representing shapes using manipulatives, drawings, and words.
- Using flips and turns to identify shapes that are congruent.
- Analyzing and classifying shapes using their properties (number of sides, corners, right angles, and lines of symmetry).
- Measuring area and perimeter.

Key Vocabulary

- congruent
- corner (vertex)
- hexagon
- line of symmetry
- pentagon
- quadrilateral

Math Facts

For item J, students illustrate multiplication number sentences.

Homework

1. Assign some of Professor Peabody's Shape Riddles.
2. Assign Home Practice Part 3.

Assessment

Students complete the *Three Tans* Assessment Pages.

Materials List

Supplies and Copies

Student	Teacher
Supplies for Each Student • scissors • centimeter ruler • plain paper to sketch shapes **Supplies for Each Student Group** • envelope for storing cutout shapes • 2 sets of tangrams	**Supplies**
Copies • 1 copy of *Four Triangles Data Tables 1* and *2* per student group, optional (*Unit Resource Guide* Pages 65–66) • 1 copy of *Tangram Pieces Master* per student group, optional (*Unit Resource Guide* Page 32) • 1 copy of *Three Tans* per student (*Unit Resource Guide* Pages 67–68)	**Copies/Transparencies** • 1 transparency of *Four Triangles Data Tables 1* and *2* (*Unit Resource Guide* Pages 65–66) • 1 transparency of *Tangram Pieces Master,* colored and cut out or 2 sets of tangram pieces (*Unit Resource Guide* Page 32)

All blackline masters including assessment, transparency, and DPP masters are also on the Teacher Resource CD.

Student Books

Building with Four Triangles (*Student Guide* Pages 170–172)

Daily Practice and Problems and Home Practice

DPP items G–J (*Unit Resource Guide* Pages 17–18)
Home Practice Part 3 (*Discovery Assignment Book* Page 179)

Note: Classrooms whose pacing differs significantly from the suggested pacing of the units should use the Math Facts Calendar in Section 4 of the *Facts Resource Guide* to ensure students receive the complete math facts program.

Daily Practice and Problems

Suggestions for using the DPPs are on page 63.

G. Bit: Subtraction (URG p. 17)

Complete the following problems. Use pencil and paper or mental math to find the answers.

1. 594
   − 225

2. 6784
   − 2387

3. 231
   − 179

4. 602
   − 199

Explain your strategy for Question 3.

H. Task: Larry the Lizard Show
(URG p. 17)

Use the Lizardland picture in the Student Guide, Unit 11, to solve the following problems. A total of 178 people attended the 10 A.M. show, whereas 284 people attended the noon show.

1. How many more people attended the noon show than the 10 A.M. show?
2. How many people attended the first two shows?
3. How many empty seats were there during the first two shows?

I. Bit: Bus Stop (URG p. 18)

Starting at 7:00 in the morning, a bus passes Ellen's stop every 15 minutes.

1. How many minutes must Ellen wait for the next bus if she gets to the stop at 9:05?
2. Will a bus come at 4:20 in the afternoon? How do you know?

J. Task: Story Solving (URG p. 18)

1. $3 \times 9 = ?$ Write a story and draw a picture about 3×9. Write a number sentence on your picture.
2. $3 \times \frac{1}{2} = ?$ Write a story, and draw a picture about $3 \times \frac{1}{2}$. Write a number sentence on your picture.

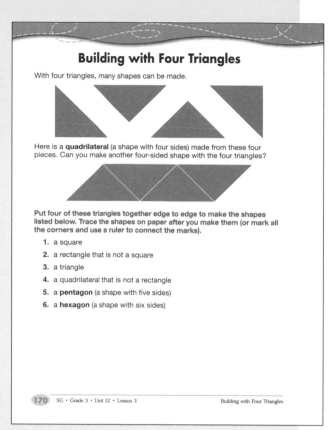

Building with Four Triangles

With four triangles, many shapes can be made.

Here is a **quadrilateral** (a shape with four sides) made from these four pieces. Can you make another four-sided shape with the four triangles?

Put four of these triangles together edge to edge to make the shapes listed below. Trace the shapes on paper after you make them (or mark all the corners and use a ruler to connect the marks).

1. a square
2. a rectangle that is not a square
3. a triangle
4. a quadrilateral that is not a rectangle
5. a **pentagon** (a shape with five sides)
6. a **hexagon** (a shape with six sides)

Student Guide - page 170 (Answers on p. 69)

Figure 14: *Fourteen ways of putting four isosceles right triangles together edge to edge*

Before the Activity

The rules and procedures in this lesson follow the working pattern established in Lesson 2 *Building with Triangles*. Please refer to that lesson for the necessary background. Each group will need four of the smallest tangram triangles and one square tangram. Provide each group with one copy of the *Tangram Pieces Master* Blackline Master or two sets of tangram pieces. If actual tangram pieces are used, they should be close to the same size as those on the *Tangram Pieces Master*.

Teaching the Activity

This lesson includes an extended investigation of shapes that can be made with four isosceles right triangles and a similar assessment exercise. Most of the activities are suitable for groups of two or three students working together.

The first page of the *Building with Four Triangles* Activity Pages describes in words some shapes for students to make using four triangles. With four triangles, there are many shapes that can be made. The first three shapes to be made—square, nonsquare rectangle, and triangle—have unique solutions, except for variations in the placement of the interior triangles. The next three shapes—nonrectangular quadrilateral, pentagon, and hexagon—have multiple nonequivalent solutions. Figure 14 shows the 14 shapes we found.

This profusion of four-triangle shapes allows plenty of room for open-ended work. We encourage you to let your students try to find as many of the fourteen possible shapes as they can.

At the same time, however, this abundance of shapes makes it difficult to organize the investigation, to have a coherent discussion, and to achieve closure. In the section Professor Peabody's Shapes, Professor Peabody comes to the rescue. Peabody has found and named all fourteen shapes, but he has failed to draw in the interior triangles. With this hint, students can track down any shapes they haven't made.

TIMS Tip

Instead of filling out a data table for their shapes, students may neatly record all measurements (using units) for each shape next to their tracings of the shapes. Then students may transfer their data to the transparencies of *Four Triangles Data Table 1* and *2*.

To investigate each of Professor Peabody's shapes, students repeat the same type of inquiries they carried out for shapes in Lesson 2. They count the number of sides, corners, and interior right angles. They also measure area and perimeter.

This task is particularly appropriate for groups of two or three students. So that each group does not have to make measurements for all fourteen shapes, assign only a few shapes to each group. Provide each group with a copy of either *Four Triangles Data Table 1* or *2,* and mark the shapes you expect each group to investigate. Students must make and trace each of their shapes on their own paper so they can make accurate measurements. Groups record their measurements on their copy of the data table, then transfer their data onto a transparency of the data table. Once all the data is collected and recorded, discuss any patterns students see.

Professor Peabody's Shapes

Professor Peabody made shapes with four triangles put together edge to edge. He used four triangles like this one.

He named his shapes and sketched the outlines, but he forgot to show the inner lines for each triangle.

drum   kite   fox   stroller   flattop
home   cat   slide
door   zigzag   wing   boat
crane   clock

7. Use four triangles to make some of Professor Peabody's shapes. Your teacher will tell you which shapes your group will make and measure. Draw the shapes on paper. Show where the inner triangles go.

8. Count the sides, corners, and right angles for each of the shapes your group is working on. Write this information down next to each shape so you can share it with your classmates.

9. Measure and record the area and perimeter of each shape. Find the perimeter to the nearest half centimeter with your ruler.

Remember, we discovered that the area of one small triangle is one square inch.

Student Guide - page 171 (Answers on p. 70)

Be ready to record your measurements in a data table like this one so you can share your data with the class.

Name of Shape	Sketch	No. of Sides	No. of Corners (vertices)	No. of Right Angles	Area (sq in)	Perimeter (cm)

10. Which of Professor Peabody's shapes have line symmetry? Draw the lines of symmetry on your sketches and in the data table.

11. Find and describe a pattern in your data. Explain why the pattern happens.

Professor Peabody's Shape Riddles

Solve Professor Peabody's riddles about his four-triangle shapes.

12. We are the only shapes with 5 sides (pentagons). Who are we?

13. I have the most right angles and the smallest perimeter. Who am I?

14. I have the fewest right angles and the largest perimeter. Who am I?

15. I am a hexagon. If you turn me halfway around, then I look the same. Who am I?

16. I have four lines of symmetry. Who am I?

17. Make up a riddle of your own. The answer to your riddle should be one or more of Professor Peabody's shapes. Use clues about symmetry, area, perimeter, number of sides, and so on. Write your riddle neatly, and write the answer in another place. Trade with a friend, and solve each other's riddles. Fix your riddle if it has a mistake.

Student Guide - page 172 (Answers on p. 71)

The next section, Professor Peabody's Shape Riddles, provides five riddles for students to solve. Then students compose their own. Solving these riddles requires logical thinking and classification by multiple variables. You can begin by working through one or two riddles as a class and then send the rest home. With your students in small groups, pose a riddle, give students a few minutes to work, then ask them to share their results and reasoning. Use the Professor Peabody's riddles or make up your own. Here are two other riddles you might ask:

- We are the only shapes with no right angle. Who are we? (slide, door, flattop)
- We have exactly one line of symmetry. Who are we? (cat, fox, wing, flattop)

Journal Prompt

Imagine that you are writing a riddle about Professor Peabody's shapes for homework, but you have forgotten your *Student Guide*. You can't remember the name of your shape. Draw your shape in your journal. Then write what you would say on the telephone to a friend so that your friend could look up the shape and tell you its name.

Math Facts

Task J develops strategies for multiplying by three.

Homework and Practice

- DPP Bit G and Task H are problems involving subtraction. Task I is a problem involving bus times.

- The Professor Peabody's Shape Riddles section is appropriate for homework. Pose and discuss several riddles in class before sending this work home. Students will need to take home their *Student Guide,* four triangles, and sketches.

- Home Practice Part 3 provides practice with multiplication and division.

Answers for Part 3 of the Home Practice are in the Answer Key at the end of this lesson and at the end of this unit.

Assessment

On the *Three Tans* Assessment Pages, students cover each of four shapes with three given tans. Students will need the three shapes and a centimeter ruler. After students identify which shapes can be covered with the three tangram pieces, they then count the sides, corners, right angles, and measure the area and perimeter of those shapes. Students record the measurements in a data table. Shapes A and D can be covered. Students should trace the three tangram pieces on these two shapes to show where each piece needs to be placed to fill the outline exactly. Shapes B and C cannot be covered. Ask students to explain why they are impossible to solve. The challenge question asks students to use three tangram pieces to find as many shapes as can be made. Students may record these shapes on a separate sheet of paper by tracing each shape they find.

Discovery Assignment Book - page 179 *(Answers on p. 71)*

At a Glance

Math Facts and Daily Practice and Problems

DPP items G and H are problems involving subtraction. Item I is a problem involving time. For item J, students illustrate multiplication number sentences.

Teaching the Activity

1. Students complete *Questions 1–6* on the *Building with Four Triangles* Activity Page. They create and trace shapes using four triangle tangram pieces.
2. Student groups are assigned some of the fourteen shapes shown in the Professor Peabody's Shapes section. They make and trace the shapes using four triangle tangram pieces and draw lines to show where the inner triangles go. *(Question 7)*
3. Students fill in the appropriate rows of *Four Triangles Data Table 1* or *2* after measuring the assigned shapes. *(Questions 8–10)*
4. Students transfer their data onto the class transparency of the data tables.
5. The class discusses any patterns found in the data shown on the overhead. *(Question 11)*
6. Students solve a few riddles in the Professor Peabody's Shape Riddles section. Assign the rest for homework. *(Questions 12–16)*
7. Students make up their own riddles to share with classmates. *(Question 17)*

Homework

1. Assign some of Professor Peabody's Shape Riddles.
2. Assign Home Practice Part 3.

Assessment

Students complete the *Three Tans* Assessment Pages.

Answer Key is on pages 69–73.

Notes:

Four Triangles Data Table 1

Name of Shape	Sketch	No. of Sides	No. of Corners (vertices)	No. of Right Angles	Area (sq in)	Perimeter (cm)
drum						
kite						
fox						
stroller						
flattop						
horse						
door						

Four Triangles Data Table 2

Name of Shape	Sketch	No. of Sides	No. of Corners (vertices)	No. of Right Angles	Area (sq in)	Perimeter (cm)
cat						
slide						
zigzag						
wing						
boat						
crane						
check						

Three Tans

1. Use the three tangram pieces that match those above to cover the shapes below.

2. If a shape can be covered exactly, draw lines inside it to show how.

3. Complete the data table for only those shapes below that can be covered.

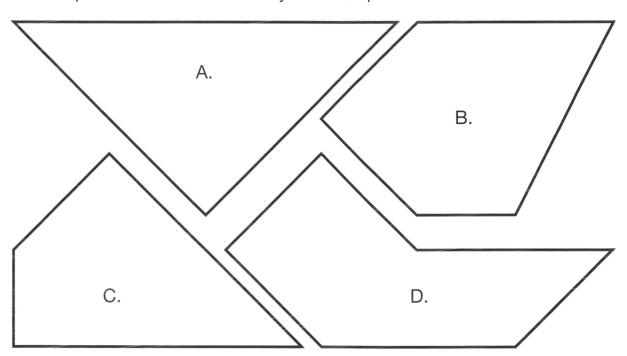

A.

B.

C.

D.

Shape	Sketch	No. of Sides	No. of Corners (vertices)	No. of Right Angles	Area (sq in)	Perimeter (cm)

4. If a shape cannot be covered, explain why in a sentence or two.

Challenge: Find all the shapes you can make by putting these three tans together edge to edge. Draw the shapes on a separate sheet of paper.

Assessment Blackline Master

Student Guide (p. 170)

The names of the shapes refer to the names Professor Peabody uses in the *Student Guide*.

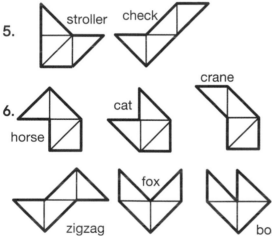

1. kite

2. drum

3. wing

4. door   slide   flattop

5. stroller   check

6. horse   cat   crane

zigzag   fox   boat

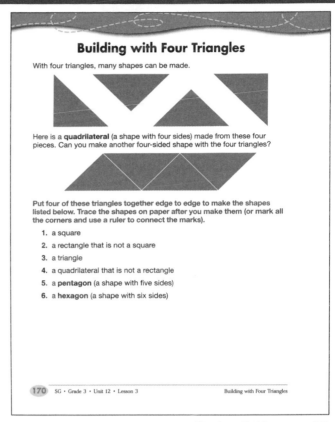

Building with Four Triangles

With four triangles, many shapes can be made.

Here is a **quadrilateral** (a shape with four sides) made from these four pieces. Can you make another four-sided shape with the four triangles?

Put four of these triangles together edge to edge to make the shapes listed below. Trace the shapes on paper after you make them (or mark all the corners and use a ruler to connect the marks).

1. a square
2. a rectangle that is not a square
3. a triangle
4. a quadrilateral that is not a rectangle
5. a **pentagon** (a shape with five sides)
6. a **hexagon** (a shape with six sides)

170   SG • Grade 3 • Unit 12 • Lesson 3   Building with Four Triangles

Student Guide - page 170

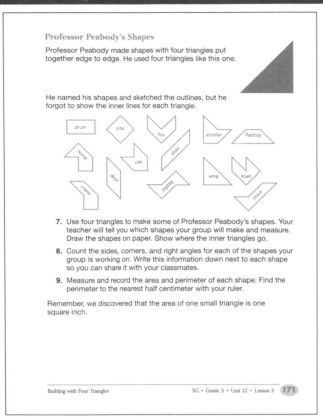

Student Guide - page 171

Student Guide (p. 171)

7. See the shapes shown for *Questions 1–6* for one way to fill in each shape.

8.–9. The names in the table refer to the names Professor Peabody uses.

Name	# Sides	# Corners	# right angle	Area (sq in)	Perimeter (cm)
drum	4	4	4	4 sq in	21 cm
kite	4	4	4	4 sq in	20 cm
fox	6	6	1	4 sq in	27 cm
stroller	5	5	1	4 sq in	24 cm
flat-top	4	4	0	4 sq in	24 cm
horse	6	6	3	4 sq in	24 cm
door	4	4	0	4 sq in	24 cm
cat	6	6	1	4 sq in	24 cm
slide	4	4	0	4 sq in	27 cm
zigzag	6	6	2	4 sq in	27 cm
wing	3	3	1	4 sq in	24 cm
boat	6	6	2	4 sq in	27 cm
crane	6	6	2	4 sq in	24 cm
check	5	5	1	4 sq in	27 cm

Student Guide (p. 172)

10.

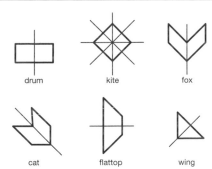

drum   kite   fox

cat   flattop   wing

11. The number of corners and the number of sides are always equal. The area is always 4 sq in because each shape is made up of 4 triangles that are each 1 sq in. Although there are 14 different shapes there are only 4 different measurements for the perimeter. Explanations will vary.

12. check and stroller

13. kite

14. slide

15. zigzag

16. kite

17. Riddles will vary.

Discovery Assignment Book (p. 179)

Home Practice*

Part 3

1. No, there are 42 people in the troop and the roller coaster can only hold 32 people.

2. 5 rides. 32 girls can ride in 4 rides but there are 3 girls left. Therefore it will take one more ride for all the girls to ride.

3. 21 bumper cars. 42 people in the group divide into 21 groups of 2.

4. A. Yes, the ride holds 45 people and there are 42 people in the group.

   B. 7 cars; 14 girls will ride with seven adults leaving 21 girls to ride without an adult. 21 is seven groups of three.

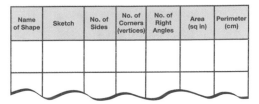

Be ready to record your measurements in a data table like this one so you can share your data with the class.

Name of Shape	Sketch	No. of Sides	No. of Corners (vertices)	No. of Right Angles	Area (sq in)	Perimeter (cm)

10. Which of Professor Peabody's shapes have line symmetry? Draw the lines of symmetry on your sketches and in the data table.

11. Find and describe a pattern in your data. Explain why the pattern happens.

Professor Peabody's Shape Riddles

Solve Professor Peabody's riddles about his four-triangle shapes.

12. We are the only shapes with 5 sides (pentagons). Who are we?

13. I have the most right angles and the smallest perimeter. Who am I?

14. I have the fewest right angles and the largest perimeter. Who am I?

15. I am a hexagon. If you turn me halfway around, then I look the same. Who am I?

16. I have four lines of symmetry. Who am I?

17. Make up a riddle of your own. The answer to your riddle should be one or more of Professor Peabody's shapes. Use clues about symmetry, area, perimeter, number of sides, and so on. Write your riddle neatly, and write the answer in another place. Trade with a friend, and solve each other's riddles. Fix your riddle if it has a mistake.

172 SG • Grade 3 • Unit 12 • Lesson 3   Building with Four Triangles

Student Guide - page 172

Name _____ Date _____

PART 3

Girl Scout Troop 903 went to Lizardland. Thirty-five girls were accompanied by seven adults. Use this information to solve the following problems:

1. The Girl Scout troop is standing in line for the Leaping Lizard roller coaster. There are 8 cars on the roller coaster and each car can hold 4 people. Can the entire group ride the roller coaster at one time? Explain.

2. If 8 people can ride the Lizard-Go-Round at the same time, how many rides will it take for all the girls to ride one time? Explain.

3. The troop is standing in line for the Bump-a-Lizard bumper cars. Each car holds 2 people. How many bumper cars will the troop need for everyone in the group? Explain.

4. The Curly-Whirly-Lizard ride fits 3 people per car. There are 15 cars on the ride.
   A. Can the entire group ride the ride at the same time? Explain.
   B. If one adult rode in a car of girls, how many cars would not have an adult?

PART 4

1. Look at the six shapes below. Draw an X on the right angle(s) inside the shapes.

2. If any of the six shapes are symmetrical, draw in the lines of symmetry that divide the shape in half.

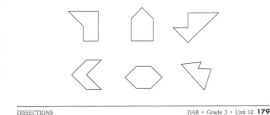

DISSECTIONS   DAB • Grade 3 • Unit 12 **179**

Discovery Assignment Book - page 179

*Answers for all the Home Practice in the *Discovery Assignment Book* are at the end of the unit.

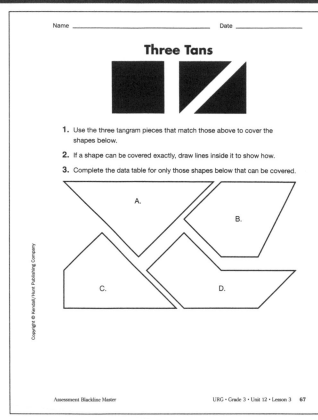

Unit Resource Guide - page 67

Unit Resource Guide (p. 67)

Three Tans

1.–2.

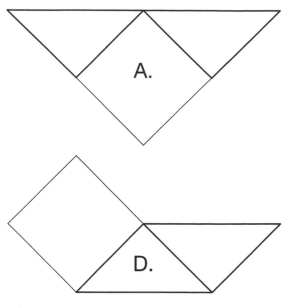

3.

Name	# Sides	# Corners	# right angle	Area sq in	Perimeter cm
A wing	3	3	1	4 sq in	24 cm
D shoe	6	6	2	4 sq in	24 cm

Unit Resource Guide (p. 68)

4. The area of shape B is correct (a fact that may escape some students), but the angles are wrong. In particular, the angle at the top right corner cannot be matched by any combination of the three given tans (or any other combination of tangram pieces). A good student response addresses these points, preferably using terms like area and angles. The area of shape C is incorrect. This shape has an area of 3.5 sq in; the three tans have a total area of 4 sq in. Hence this shape cannot be covered exactly without overlapping the three tans.

Challenge:

This problem requires a systematic search. To see that the following shapes are all that can be made, note first that the square and the first triangle can be joined in only one way. There are then five edges where the second triangle can be added. On four of these edges, the second triangle can be joined in two ways. Eliminating shapes obtained in more than one way yields the eight shapes below.

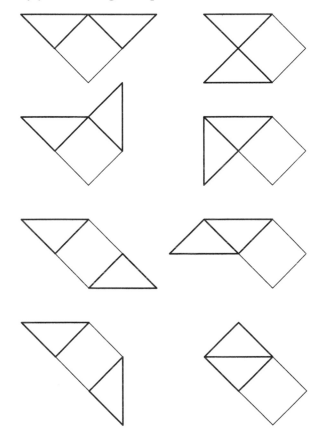

| Name _____ | Date _____ |

Shape	Sketch	No. of Sides	No. of Corners (vertices)	No. of Right Angles	Area (sq in)	Perimeter (cm)

4. If a shape cannot be covered, explain why in a sentence or two.

Challenge: Find all the shapes you can make by putting these three tans together edge to edge. Draw the shapes on a separate sheet of paper.

Assessment Blackline Master

Unit Resource Guide - page 68

Lesson 4

Dissection Puzzles

Lesson Overview

Students solve puzzles that require dissecting figures in specific ways. In each puzzle, they put together a set of pieces edge to edge to make various shapes. Three such puzzles are included for use now; similar puzzles will appear in the Daily Practice and Problems.

Key Content

- Representing shapes with manipulatives, drawings, and words.
- Developing spatial visualization skills.
- Using geometric concepts and skills.

Math Facts

DPP Bit K provides practice with the multiplication facts for the threes.

Homework

1. Puzzles may be assigned for homework.
2. Assign Home Practice Part 4.

Assessment

1. Puzzle C provides an opportunity to observe students' abilities to analyze and describe two-dimensional shapes. Record your observations on the *Observational Assessment Record*.
2. Transfer information from the Unit 12 *Observational Assessment Record* to students' *Individual Assessment Record Sheets*.

Materials List

Supplies and Copies

Student	Teacher
Supplies for Each Student • scissors • set of tangram pieces, optional	**Supplies**
Copies	**Copies/Transparencies**

All blackline masters including assessment, transparency, and DPP masters are also on the Teacher Resource CD.

Student Books
Dissection Puzzles (*Student Guide* Pages 173–175)
Puzzle Pieces (*Discovery Assignment Book* Page 189)

Daily Practice and Problems and Home Practice
DPP items K–L (*Unit Resource Guide* Pages 18–19)
Home Practice Part 4 (*Discovery Assignment Book* Page 179)

Note: Classrooms whose pacing differs significantly from the suggested pacing of the units should use the Math Facts Calendar in Section 4 of the *Facts Resource Guide* to ensure students receive the complete math facts program.

Assessment Tools
Observational Assessment Record (*Unit Resource Guide* Pages 11–12)
Individual Assessment Record Sheet (*Teacher Implementation Guide,* Assessment section)

Daily Practice and Problems

Suggestions for using the DPPs are on page 78.

K. Bit: Using Threes (URG p. 18)

Do these problems in your head. Write only the answers.

A. $3 \times 5 =$ B. $7 \times 3 =$
C. $9 \times 3 =$ D. $3 \times 2 =$
E. $10 \times 3 =$ F. $3 \times 6 =$
G. $4 \times 3 =$ H. $3 \times 3 =$
I. $3 \times 1 =$ J. $8 \times 3 =$

Describe a strategy for 8×3.

L. Task: Dissection Puzzle 1 (URG p. 19)

Trace and cut out the following triangles.

1. Put them edge to edge to make a rectangle.
2. Put them edge to edge to make a triangle.
3. Make four other shapes.

76   URG • Grade 3 • Unit 12 • Lesson 4

These puzzles are variations on the themes that have been explored extensively in Lesson 1 *Tangrams* and Lesson 2 *Building with Triangles*. These puzzles can be used in many ways. All are suitable for homework. You can use the last one (Puzzle C) for assessment.

Students cut out puzzle pieces from the *Puzzle Pieces* Activity Page in the *Discovery Assignment Book*. The three puzzles on the *Dissection Puzzles* Activity Pages in the *Student Guide* prepare students for those they will encounter later in the Daily Practice and Problems.

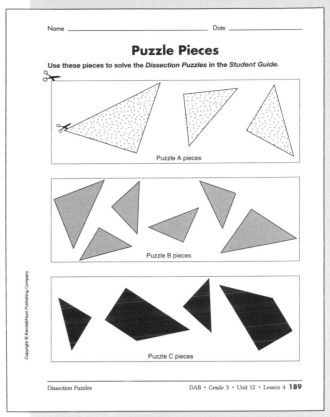

Name _____ Date _____

Puzzle Pieces

Use these pieces to solve the *Dissection Puzzles* in the *Student Guide.*

Puzzle A pieces

Puzzle B pieces

Puzzle C pieces

Dissection Puzzles   DAB • Grade 3 • Unit 12 • Lesson 4 **189**

Discovery Assignment Book - page 189

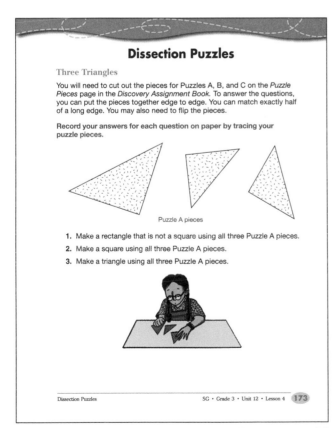

Dissection Puzzles

Three Triangles

You will need to cut out the pieces for Puzzles A, B, and C on the *Puzzle Pieces* page in the *Discovery Assignment Book*. To answer the questions, you can put the pieces together edge to edge. You can match exactly half of a long edge. You may also need to flip the pieces.

Record your answers for each question on paper by tracing your puzzle pieces.

Puzzle A pieces

1. Make a rectangle that is not a square using all three Puzzle A pieces.
2. Make a square using all three Puzzle A pieces.
3. Make a triangle using all three Puzzle A pieces.

Dissection Puzzles   SG • Grade 3 • Unit 12 • Lesson 4 **173**

Student Guide - page 173 (Answers on p. 81)

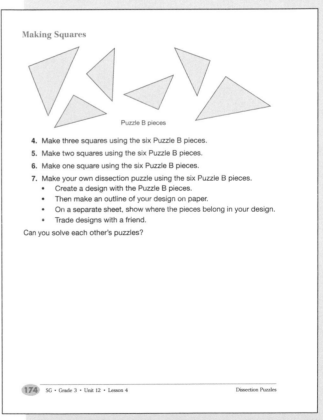

Making Squares

Puzzle B pieces

4. Make three squares using the six Puzzle B pieces.
5. Make two squares using the six Puzzle B pieces.
6. Make one square using the six Puzzle B pieces.
7. Make your own dissection puzzle using the six Puzzle B pieces.
   • Create a design with the Puzzle B pieces.
   • Then make an outline of your design on paper.
   • On a separate sheet, show where the pieces belong in your design.
   • Trade designs with a friend.

Can you solve each other's puzzles?

174 SG • Grade 3 • Unit 12 • Lesson 4   Dissection Puzzles

Student Guide - page 174 (Answers on p. 81)

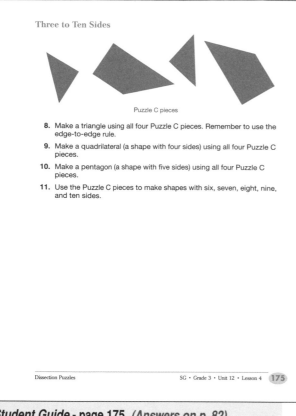

Three to Ten Sides

Puzzle C pieces

8. Make a triangle using all four Puzzle C pieces. Remember to use the edge-to-edge rule.

9. Make a quadrilateral (a shape with four sides) using all four Puzzle C pieces.

10. Make a pentagon (a shape with five sides) using all four Puzzle C pieces.

11. Use the Puzzle C pieces to make shapes with six, seven, eight, nine, and ten sides.

Dissection Puzzles   SG • Grade 3 • Unit 12 • Lesson 4   175

Student Guide - page 175 *(Answers on p. 82)*

As students try to solve Puzzles A and B, you can provide hints. Tell them that two smaller triangles can be put together edge to edge to form the larger triangle in both puzzle piece sets A and B. Also remind them that they may flip the pieces if necessary. After students solve the puzzles, they should trace their pieces on paper to show their solutions. Encourage them to share their solutions.

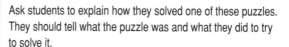

TIMS Tip

Students may use the tangram pieces instead of puzzle pieces A and B. To solve puzzle B, however, they need two sets of tangram pieces. They need four small triangles and two mid-size tangram triangles. If each student is given one set, student pairs can work together to solve Puzzle B. Students must, however, cut out Puzzle C pieces to complete *Questions 8–11.*

Journal Prompt

Ask students to explain how they solved one of these puzzles. They should tell what the puzzle was and what they did to try to solve it.

Math Facts

DPP Bit K develops strategies for learning the multiplication facts for the threes.

Homework and Practice

• DPP Task L is a dissection puzzle.

• All of the puzzles on the *Dissection Puzzles* Activity Pages are suitable for homework. Students need the *Puzzle Pieces* Activity Page from the *Discovery Assignment Book* to complete the puzzles.

• Home Practice Part 4 provides practice with some of the geometry concepts in this unit.

Answers for Part 4 of the Home Practice are in the Answer Key at the end of this lesson and at the end of this unit.

Assessment

These puzzles can provide useful information about students' geometric understanding and communication skills. Puzzle C has both well-defined problems and open-ended investigations, so this one may be more useful for assessment than Puzzles A or B. Use the *Observational Assessment Record* to record students' abilities to analyze and describe two-dimensional shapes and to communicate their reasoning.

Extension

Ask students what other shapes they can make with the Puzzle A pieces after completing *Questions 1–3* in the *Student Guide*. Ask them to make as many shapes as they can. Students can trace their solutions on a piece of paper and share their solutions with the class.

Name _____ Date _____

Copyright © Kendall/Hunt Publishing Company

PART 3

Girl Scout Troop 903 went to Lizardland. Thirty-five girls were accompanied by seven adults. Use this information to solve the following problems:

1. The Girl Scout troop is standing in line for the Leaping Lizard roller coaster. There are 8 cars on the roller coaster and each car can hold 4 people. Can the entire group ride the roller coaster at one time? Explain.

2. If 8 people can ride the Lizard-Go-Round at the same time, how many rides will it take for all the girls to ride one time? Explain.

3. The troop is standing in line for the Bump-a-Lizard bumper cars. Each car holds 2 people. How many bumper cars will the troop need for everyone in the group? Explain.

4. The Curly-Whirly-Lizard ride fits 3 people per car. There are 15 cars on the ride.
   A. Can the entire group ride the ride at the same time? Explain.
   B. If one adult rode in a car of girls, how many cars would not have an adult?

PART 4

1. Look at the six shapes below. Draw an **X** on the right angle(s) inside the shapes.

2. If any of the six shapes are symmetrical, draw in the lines of symmetry that divide the shape in half.

DISSECTIONS

DAB • Grade 3 • Unit 12 **179**

Discovery Assignment Book - page 179 (Answers on p. 83)

At a Glance

Math Facts and Daily Practice and Problems

DPP Bit K provides practice with the multiplication facts for the threes and DPP Task L is a dissection puzzle.

Teaching the Activity

1. Students cut out the pieces for Puzzles A, B, and C from the *Puzzle Pieces* Activity Page in the *Discovery Assignment Book*.
2. Students complete the *Dissection Puzzles* Activity Pages in the *Student Guide*. They trace their solutions on paper.
3. Students share their solutions.

Homework

1. Puzzles may be assigned for homework.
2. Assign Home Practice Part 4.

Assessment

1. Puzzle C provides an opportunity to observe students' abilities to analyze and describe two-dimensional shapes. Record your observations on the *Observational Assessment Record*.
2. Transfer information from the Unit 12 *Observational Assessment Record* to students' *Individual Assessment Record Sheets*.

Extension

Challenge students to find what other shapes they can make with Puzzle A pieces.

Answer Key is on pages 81–83.

Notes:

Student Guide (p. 173)

Dissection Puzzles

1.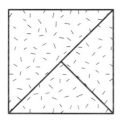

2.

3.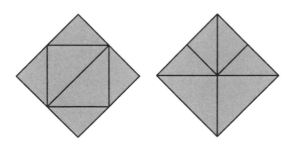

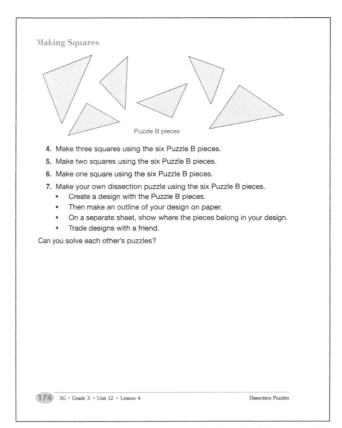

Student Guide - page 173

Student Guide (p. 174)

4.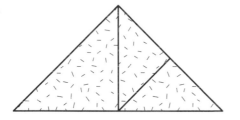

5.

6. Answers will vary. Two solutions are shown below.

7. Answers will vary.

Three to Ten Sides

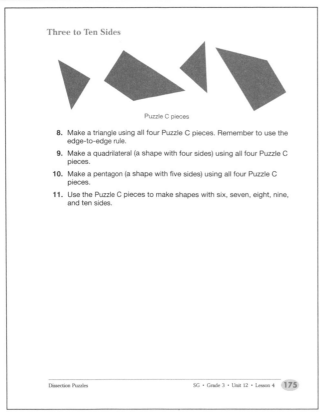

Puzzle C pieces

8. Make a triangle using all four Puzzle C pieces. Remember to use the edge-to-edge rule.

9. Make a quadrilateral (a shape with four sides) using all four Puzzle C pieces.

10. Make a pentagon (a shape with five sides) using all four Puzzle C pieces.

11. Use the Puzzle C pieces to make shapes with six, seven, eight, nine, and ten sides.

Dissection Puzzles   SG • Grade 3 • Unit 12 • Lesson 4   175

Student Guide - page 175

10. Answers will vary.

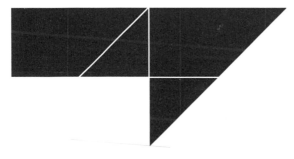

11. Answers will vary. The following is an example of a shape with seven sides.

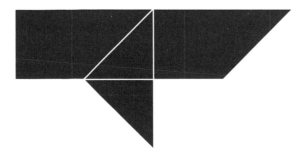

Student Guide (p. 175)

8. One solution is shown below.

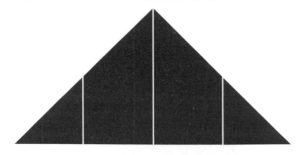

9. Answers will vary. Three solutions are shown below.

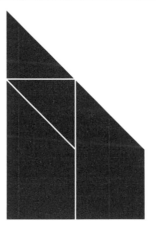

*Answers and/or discussion are included in the Lesson Guide.

Discovery Assignment Book (p. 179)

Home Practice*

Part 4

1.–2.

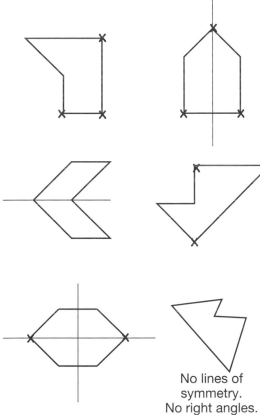

No lines of
symmetry.
No right angles.

Name _____ Date _____

PART 3

Girl Scout Troop 903 went to Lizardland. Thirty-five girls were accompanied by seven adults. Use this information to solve the following problems:

1. The Girl Scout troop is standing in line for the Leaping Lizard roller coaster. There are 8 cars on the roller coaster and each car can hold 4 people. Can the entire group ride the roller coaster at one time? Explain.

2. If 8 people can ride the Lizard-Go-Round at the same time, how many rides will it take for all the girls to ride one time? Explain.

3. The troop is standing in line for the Bump-a-Lizard bumper cars. Each car holds 2 people. How many bumper cars will the troop need for everyone in the group? Explain.

4. The Curly-Whirly-Lizard ride fits 3 people per car. There are 15 cars on the ride.
   A. Can the entire group ride the ride at the same time? Explain.
   B. If one adult rode in a car of girls, how many cars would not have an adult?

PART 4

1. Look at the six shapes below. Draw an **X** on the right angle(s) inside the shapes.

2. If any of the six shapes are symmetrical, draw in the lines of symmetry that divide the shape in half.

DISSECTIONS   DAB • Grade 3 • Unit 12 **179**

Discovery Assignment Book - page 179

---

*Answers for all the Home Practice in the *Discovery Assignment Book* are at the end of the unit.

Lesson 5

Hex

Estimated Class Sessions

1

Lesson Overview

Students play a geometric game similar to tic-tac-toe or "boxes." In later units, this game will be adapted to provide practice in estimation and mental computation.

Key Content

• Reasoning logically and strategically in a game situation.

Math Facts

DPP Bit M is a quiz on the twos and threes multiplication facts.

Homework

1. Encourage students to play *Hex* with a family member.
2. Assign the word problems in Lesson 6 for homework.

Assessment

DPP Bit M is a quiz to assess the twos and threes multiplication facts.

Materials List

Supplies and Copies

Student	Teacher
Supplies for Each Student Pair • 25 of each of two kinds of beans or other small markers	**Supplies**
Copies	**Copies/Transparencies** • 1 transparency of *4-by-4 Hex*, optional (*Unit Resource Guide* Page 89)

All blackline masters including assessment, transparency, and DPP masters are also on the Teacher Resource CD.

Student Books
Hex (*Discovery Assignment Book* Page 191)

Daily Practice and Problems and Home Practice
DPP items M–N (*Unit Resource Guide* Pages 19–20)

Note: Classrooms whose pacing differs significantly from the suggested pacing of the units should use the Math Facts Calendar in Section 4 of the *Facts Resource Guide* to ensure students receive the complete math facts program.

M. Bit: Quiz on 2s and 3s (URG p. 19)

A. $4 \times 2 =$	B. $3 \times 2 =$
C. $5 \times 3 =$	D. $2 \times 10 =$
E. $6 \times 3 =$	F. $2 \times 5 =$
G. $10 \times 3 =$	H. $7 \times 2 =$
I. $8 \times 3 =$	J. $3 \times 3 =$
K. $8 \times 2 =$	L. $2 \times 2 =$
M. $9 \times 2 =$	N. $6 \times 2 =$
O. $3 \times 7 =$	P. $4 \times 3 =$
Q. $3 \times 9 =$	R. $3 \times 1 =$

N. Challenge: Dissection Puzzle 2
(URG p. 20)

1. Trace and cut out the shapes below.

2. Find all shapes that can be made by putting the three pieces edge to edge. Trace them on a piece of paper.

3. Make a data table that shows the area, perimeter, and lines of symmetry for each shape.

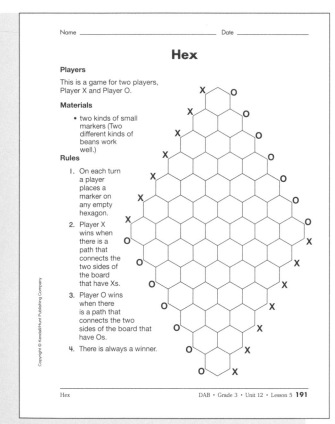

Discovery Assignment Book - page 191

Teaching the Game

As outlined on the *Hex* Game Page in the *Discovery Assignment Book,* players take turns placing one marker on a hexagon. Player X goes first and tries to make a path that connects the two sides of the board that have Xs. Player O tries to make a path that connects the two sides of the board that have Os. Figure 15 shows a game on a smaller board in which Player X went first, using black beans and Player O used white beans.

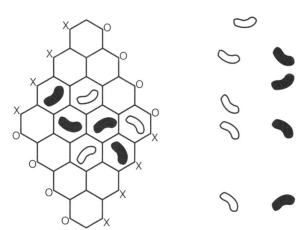

Figure 15: *A win for Player X*

One way to introduce this game is to play against one of your students using a transparency of the *4-by-4 Hex* Transparency Master. The transparency allows for a short game. The regular version has a 7-by-7 array of hexagons.

After the rules are clear, students can play in pairs several times. In later units, variations of this game will involve estimation and mental arithmetic. The game board will be similar but numbers will be located on the hexagons. Students will use estimation to select two numbers that will help them make a path from one side of the game board to the other.

Homework and Practice

- DPP Challenge N is a dissection puzzle. Encourage students to share their solutions.
- Students can play *Hex* at home with a family member. They will need the *Hex* Game Page in the *Discovery Assignment Book*.
- Assign some or all of the word problems in Lesson 6 *Focus on Word Problems* for homework.

Assessment

DPP Bit M is a quiz on the twos and threes multiplication facts.

Extension

An interesting question is whether the player who goes first, Player X, wins more often than the other player and, if so, why. If Player X always plays first and students tally game outcomes in a data table like the one in Figure 16, then a pattern may emerge.

Player	Wins	
	Tallies	Total
X		
O		

Figure 16: *Table for analyzing whether Player X wins more often*

Math Facts and Daily Practice and Problems

DPP Bit M is a quiz on the twos and threes multiplication facts. DPP Challenge N is a dissection puzzle.

Teaching the Game

1. Introduce the game *Hex* by playing against a student using the *4-by-4 Hex* Transparency Master.
2. Students in pairs play the game several times.

Homework

1. Encourage students to play *Hex* with a family member.
2. Assign the word problems in Lesson 6 for homework.

Assessment

DPP Bit M is a quiz to assess the twos and threes multiplication facts.

Extension

Have students determine if it is an advantage to go first.

Notes:

4-by-4 Hex

Optional Lesson 6

Focus on Word Problems

Lesson Overview

Students solve a set of word problems and share their solutions and strategies.

Key Content

- Solving multistep word problems.
- Solving problems involving addition, subtraction, multiplication, and division.
- Choosing to find an estimate or an exact answer.
- Communicating solutions in writing.

Homework

Assign some or all of the problems for homework.

Supplies and Copies

Student	Teacher
Supplies for Each Student • ruler	**Supplies**
Copies • 1 copy of *Centimeter Graph Paper* per student (*Unit Resource Guide* Page 94)	**Copies/Transparencies**

All blackline masters including assessment, transparency, and DPP masters are also on the Teacher Resource CD.

Student Books

Focus on Word Problems (*Student Guide* Pages 176–177)

Focus on Word Problems

Solve the following problems. Show how you found each answer. You will need a ruler and a copy of *Centimeter Graph Paper* to complete Question 8.

1. One Saturday, 37 people volunteered to help restore a prairie. The team leader wanted to place at least 5 people on each team.
   A. How many teams were there?
   B. How many people were on each team?

2. Mrs. Hix is planning for Girl Scout Camp. Each troop can send 15 members. There are 15 troops coming to camp. About how many Girl Scouts can she expect at camp? Explain your solution.

3. The Girl Scouts are going to Springfield to visit the state capitol. There are 23 girls in the troop. Each car can carry no more than three girls and a driver. How many cars are needed? Explain how you know.

4. Beverly collected 728 pennies. She sorted them into 3 jars. Which jar would you choose if she let you keep one? Explain why you chose that jar.
   A. The first jar had as many pennies as the "2" stands for in 728.
   B. The second jar had as many pennies as the "7" stands for in 728.
   C. The third jar had as many pennies as the "8" stands for in 728.

5. Write a story for this multiplication sentence: $24 \times 3 = ?$

6. Jenny measured the perimeter of a quadrilateral (a shape with four sides). Two sides were 8 centimeters long each. The other two sides were 19 centimeters long each. What is the perimeter of the quadrilateral? Write a number sentence to show how you solved the problem.

7. Max found the mass of a box of crayons. He used ten 20-gram masses, five 10-gram masses, one 5-gram mass, and three 1-gram masses. What is the mass of the box of crayons?

 SG • Grade 3 • Unit 12 • Lesson 6   Focus on Word Problems

Student Guide - page 176 *(Answers on p. 95)*

---

8. Caroline loves fruit. She eats four pieces of fruit every day.
   A. Copy her data table on a separate sheet of paper and fill in the missing data.

D Number of Days	F Pieces of Fruit
1	4
2	8
3	
4	

   B. Graph Caroline's data on a sheet of *Centimeter Graph Paper*.
   C. How many pieces of fruit will Caroline eat in 9 days? Show how you found your answer on the graph.

9. Mrs. Reynold's class collected aluminum cans for the recycling drive. On Monday they had 436 cans. By Friday they had 712 cans. How many cans did they add to their collection between Monday and Friday?

10. This summer Fred and his father took a road trip. During the first week they traveled 487 miles. During the second week they traveled 346 miles. During their last week they traveled 279 miles.
    A. During the three weeks, estimate if they traveled more or less than 1000 miles.
    B. How many miles did Fred and his father actually drive?

Focus on Word Problems   SG • Grade 3 • Unit 12 • Lesson 6   177

Student Guide - page 177 *(Answers on p. 96)*

Students can work on these problems individually, in pairs, or in groups. Students may complete them all at once or you can distribute them throughout the unit. Students must decide when it is appropriate to estimate and when it is appropriate to find an exact answer.

Homework and Practice

Assign some or all of the problems for homework.

Extension

Ask students to write their own problems. Have students swap problems with a partner. After students solve their partners' problems, they can check each other's solutions and strategies.

At a Glance

Teaching the Activity

1. Students solve the problems on the *Focus on Word Problems* Activity Pages in the *Student Guide.*
2. Students discuss their solution strategies with the class.

Homework

Assign some or all of the problems for homework.

Extension

Ask students to write their own problems and trade problems with a partner.

Answer Key is on pages 95–96.

Notes:

Centimeter Graph Paper, Blackline Master

Student Guide (p. 176)

Focus on Word Problems

1. **A.** 7 teams

   B. 5 teams of 5 people and 2 teams of 6 people

2. Students need only an estimate. One possible strategy: $10 \times 15 = 150$ and $20 \times 15 = 300$, so there will be between 150 and 300 scouts at camp or about 200 scouts.

3. $23 \div 3 = 7$ with 2 left over; 8 cars*

4. B; Jar 1 has 20 pennies, Jar 2 has 700 pennies, Jar 3 has 8 pennies

5. Answers will vary.

6. $19 + 19 + 8 + 8 = 54$ centimeters

7. $10 \times 20 = 200$; $5 \times 10 = 50$; $1 \times 5 = 5$; $3 \times 1 = 3$; $200 + 50 + 5 + 3 = 258$ grams

---

Focus on Word Problems

Solve the following problems. Show how you found each answer. You will need a ruler and a copy of *Centimeter Graph Paper* to complete Question 8.

1. One Saturday, 37 people volunteered to help restore a prairie. The team leader wanted to place at least 5 people on each team.
   A. How many teams were there?
   B. How many people were on each team?

2. Mrs. Hix is planning for Girl Scout Camp. Each troop can send 15 members. There are 15 troops coming to camp. About how many Girl Scouts can she expect at camp? Explain your solution.

3. The Girl Scouts are going to Springfield to visit the state capitol. There are 23 girls in the troop. Each car can carry no more than three girls and a driver. How many cars are needed? Explain how you know.

4. Beverly collected 728 pennies. She sorted them into 3 jars. Which jar would you choose if she let you keep one? Explain why you chose that jar.
   A. The first jar had as many pennies as the "2" stands for in 728.
   B. The second jar had as many pennies as the "7" stands for in 728.
   C. The third jar had as many pennies as the "8" stands for in 728.

5. Write a story for this multiplication sentence: $24 \times 3 = ?$

6. Jenny measured the perimeter of a quadrilateral (a shape with four sides). Two sides were 8 centimeters long each. The other two sides were 19 centimeters long each. What is the perimeter of the quadrilateral? Write a number sentence to show how you solved the problem.

7. Max found the mass of a box of crayons. He used ten 20-gram masses, five 10-gram masses, one 5-gram mass, and three 1-gram masses. What is the mass of the box of crayons?

Focus on Word Problems

Student Guide - **page 176**

---

*Answers and/or discussion are included in the Lesson Guide.

8. Caroline loves fruit. She eats four pieces of fruit every day.

A. Copy her data table on a separate sheet of paper and fill in the missing data.

D Number of Days	F Pieces of Fruit
1	4
2	8
3	
4	

B. Graph Caroline's data on a sheet of *Centimeter Graph Paper*.

C. How many pieces of fruit will Caroline eat in 9 days? Show how you found your answer on the graph.

9. Mrs. Reynold's class collected aluminum cans for the recycling drive. On Monday they had 436 cans. By Friday they had 712 cans. How many cans did they add to their collection between Monday and Friday?

10. This summer Fred and his father took a road trip. During the first week they traveled 487 miles. During the second week they traveled 346 miles. During their last week they traveled 279 miles.

A. During the three weeks, estimate if they traveled more or less than 1000 miles.

B. How many miles did Fred and his father actually drive?

Student Guide - page 177

Student Guide (p. 177)

8. A.

D Number of Days	F Pieces of Fruit
1	4
2	8
3	12
4	16

B.–C.

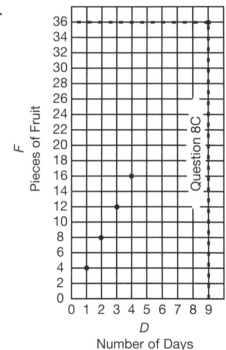

9. $712 - 436 = 276$ cans

10. A. more

B. $487 + 346 + 279 = 1112$ miles

Discovery Assignment Book (p.178)

Part 1

1. 585

2. 603

3. 472

4. 382

5. Possible strategy: 872 is close to 900 and 490 is close to 500. So the answer is close to 900 − 500 = 400.

6. 252 marbles

Part 2

1. 142

2. 201

3. 247

4. 249

5. Possible strategy: 280 − 30 = 250 and 250 − 3 = 247.

6. **A.** Yes; 40 + 20 = 60; 43 and 29 are greater than 40 and 20

   B. 72 minutes or 1 hour and 12 minutes

Name _____ Date _____

Unit 12 Home Practice

PART 1

Estimate to be sure your answers are reasonable.

1. 285
   +300

2. 285
   +318

3. 872
   −400

4. 872
   −490

5. Explain your estimation strategy for Question 4.

6. Marie has 748 marbles in her collection. She wants 1000. How many more marbles does she need?

PART 2

1. 115
   +27

2. 127
   +74

3. 280
   −33

4. 325
   −76

5. Explain a strategy for using mental math for Question 3.

6. Ted read a book for 43 minutes on Saturday and 29 minutes on Sunday.
   A. Did Ted read for more than one hour? Explain how you know.

   B. How many minutes did Ted read? _____

 DISSECTIONS

Discovery Assignment Book - page 178

Copyright © Kendall/Hunt Publishing Company

Name _____ **Date** _____

PART 3

Girl Scout Troop 903 went to Lizardland. Thirty-five girls were accompanied by seven adults. Use this information to solve the following problems:

1. The Girl Scout troop is standing in line for the Leaping Lizard roller coaster. There are 8 cars on the roller coaster and each car can hold 4 people. Can the entire group ride the roller coaster at one time? Explain.

2. If 8 people can ride the Lizard-Go-Round at the same time, how many rides will it take for all the girls to ride one time? Explain.

3. The troop is standing in line for the Bump-a-Lizard bumper cars. Each car holds 2 people. How many bumper cars will the troop need for everyone in the group? Explain.

4. The Curly-Whirly-Lizard ride fits 3 people per car. There are 15 cars on the ride.
   A. Can the entire group ride the ride at the same time? Explain.
   B. If one adult rode in a car of girls, how many cars would not have an adult?

PART 4

1. Look at the six shapes below. Draw an **X** on the right angle(s) inside the shapes.

2. If any of the six shapes are symmetrical, draw in the lines of symmetry that divide the shape in half.

DISSECTIONS   DAB • Grade 3 • Unit 12 **179**

Discovery Assignment Book - **page 179**

Discovery Assignment Book (p. 179)

Part 3

1. No, there are 42 people in the troop and the roller coaster can only hold 32 people.

2. 5 rides. 32 girls can ride in 4 rides but there are 3 girls left. Therefore it will take one more ride for all the girls to ride.

3. 21 bumper cars. 42 people in the group divide into 21 groups of 2.

4. A. Yes, the ride holds 45 people and there are 42 people in the group.

   B. 7 cars; 14 girls will ride with seven adults leaving 21 girls to ride without an adult. 21 is seven groups of three.

Part 4

1.–2.

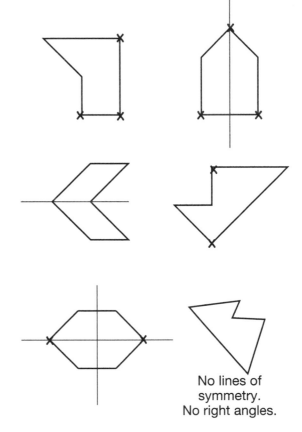

No lines of symmetry.
No right angles.

Glossary

This glossary provides definitions of key vocabulary terms in the Grade 3 lessons. Locations of key vocabulary terms in the curriculum are included with each definition. Components Key: URG = *Unit Resource Guide,* SG = *Student Guide,* and DAB = *Discovery Assignment Book.*

A

Area (URG Unit 5; SG Unit 5)
The area of a shape is the amount of space it covers, measured in square units.

Array (URG Unit 7 & Unit 11)
An array is an arrangement of elements into a rectangular pattern of (horizontal) rows and (vertical) columns. (*See* column and row.)

Associative Property of Addition (URG Unit 2)
For any three numbers a, b, and c we have $a + (b + c) = (a + b) + c$. For example in finding the sum of 4, 8, and 2, one can compute $4 + 8$ first and then add 2: $(4 + 8) + 2 = 14$. Alternatively, we can compute $8 + 2$ and then add the result to 4: $4 + (8 + 2) = 4 + 10 = 14$.

Average (URG Unit 5)
A number that can be used to represent a typical value in a set of data. (*See also* mean and median.)

Axes (URG Unit 8; SG Unit 8)
Reference lines on a graph. In the Cartesian coordinate system, the axes are two perpendicular lines that meet at the origin. The singular of axes is axis.

B

Base (of a cube model) (URG Unit 18; SG Unit 18)
The part of a cube model that sits on the "ground."

Base-Ten Board (URG Unit 4)
A tool to help children organize base-ten pieces when they are representing numbers.

Base-Ten Pieces (URG Unit 4; SG Unit 4)
A set of manipulatives used to model our number system as shown in the figure at the right. Note that a skinny is made of 10 bits, a flat is made of 100 bits, and a pack is made of 1000 bits.

Base-Ten Shorthand (SG Unit 4)
A pictorial representation of the base-ten pieces as shown.

Nickname	Picture	Shorthand
bit	⬜	·
skinny	▭	/
flat	▱	⬜
pack	▢	⬜

Best-Fit Line (URG Unit 9; SG Unit 9; DAB Unit 9)
The line that comes closest to the most number of points on a point graph.

Bit (URG Unit 4; SG Unit 4)
A cube that measures 1 cm on each edge. It is the smallest of the base-ten pieces that is often used to represent 1. (*See also* base-ten pieces.)

C

Capacity (URG Unit 16)
1. The volume of the inside of a container.
2. The largest volume a container can hold.

Cartesian Coordinate System (URG Unit 8)
A method of locating points on a flat surface by means of numbers. This method is named after its originator, René Descartes. (*See also* coordinates.)

Centimeter (cm)
A unit of measure in the metric system equal to one-hundredth of a meter. (1 inch = 2.54 cm)

Column (URG Unit 11)
In an array, the objects lined up vertically.

column 3

Common Fraction (URG Unit 15)
Any fraction that is written with a numerator and denominator that are whole numbers. For example, $\frac{3}{4}$ and $\frac{9}{4}$ are both common fractions. (*See also* decimal fraction.)

Commutative Property of Addition (URG Unit 2 & Unit 11)
This is also known as the Order Property of Addition. Changing the order of the addends does not change the sum. For example, $3 + 5 = 5 + 3 = 8$. Using variables, $n + m = m + n$.

Commutative Property of Multiplication (URG Unit 11)
Changing the order of the factors in a multiplication problem does not change the result, e.g., $7 \times 3 = 3 \times 7 = 21$. (*See also* turn-around facts.)

Congruent (URG Unit 12 & Unit 17; SG Unit 12)
Figures with the same shape and size.

Convenient Number (URG Unit 6)
A number used in computation that is close enough to give a good estimate, but is also easy to compute mentally, e.g., 25 and 30 are convenient numbers for 27.

Coordinates (URG Unit 8; SG Unit 8)
An ordered pair of numbers that locates points on a flat surface by giving distances from a pair of coordinate axes. For example, if a point has coordinates (4, 5) it is 4 units from the vertical axis and 5 units from the horizontal axis.

Counting Back (URG Unit 2)
A strategy for subtracting in which students start from a larger number and then count down until the number is reached. For example, to solve $8 - 3$, begin with 8 and count down three, 7, 6, 5.

Counting Down (*See* counting back.)

Counting Up (URG Unit 2)
A strategy for subtraction in which the student starts at the lower number and counts on to the higher number. For example, to solve $8 - 5$, the student starts at 5 and counts up three numbers (6, 7, 8). So $8 - 5 = 3$.

Cube (SG Unit 18)
A three-dimensional shape with six congruent square faces.

Cubic Centimeter (cc) (URG Unit 16; SG Unit 16)
The volume of a cube that is one centimeter long on each edge.

1 cm
1 cm
1 cm
cubic centimeter

Cup (URG Unit 16)
A unit of volume equal to 8 fluid ounces, one-half pint.

D

Decimal Fraction (URG Unit 15)
A fraction written as a decimal. For example, 0.75 and 0.4 are decimal fractions and $\frac{75}{100}$ and $\frac{4}{10}$ are called common fractions. (*See also* fraction.)

Denominator (URG Unit 13)
The number below the line in a fraction. The denominator indicates the number of equal parts in which the unit whole is divided. For example, the 5 is the denominator in the fraction $\frac{2}{5}$. In this case the unit whole is divided into five equal parts.

Density (URG Unit 16)
The ratio of an object's mass to its volume.

Difference (URG Unit 2)
The answer to a subtraction problem.

Dissection (URG Unit 12 & Unit 17)
Cutting or decomposing a geometric shape into smaller shapes that cover it exactly.

Distributive Property of Multiplication over Addition (URG Unit 19)
For any three numbers $a, b,$ and $c, a \times (b + c) = a \times b + a \times c$. The distributive property is the foundation for most methods of multidigit multiplication. For example, $9 \times (17) = 9 \times (10 + 7) = 9 \times 10 + 9 \times 7 = 90 + 63 = 153$.

E

Equal-Arm Balance
See two-pan balance.

Equilateral Triangle (URG Unit 7)
A triangle with all sides of equal length and all angles of equal measure.

Equivalent Fractions (SG Unit 17)
Fractions that have the same value, e.g., $\frac{2}{4} = \frac{1}{2}$.

Estimate (URG Unit 5 & Unit 6)
1. (verb) To find *about* how many.
2. (noun) An approximate number.

Extrapolation (URG Unit 7)
Using patterns in data to make predictions or to estimate values that lie beyond the range of values in the set of data.

F

Fact Family (URG Unit 11; SG Unit 11)
Related math facts, e.g., $3 \times 4 = 12$, $4 \times 3 = 12$, $12 \div 3 = 4$, $12 \div 4 = 3$.

Factor (URG Unit 11; SG Unit 11)
1. In a multiplication problem, the numbers that are multiplied together. In the problem $3 \times 4 = 12$, 3 and 4 are the factors.
2. Whole numbers that can be multiplied together to get a number. That is, numbers that divide a number evenly, e.g., 1, 2, 3, 4, 6, and 12 are all the factors of 12.

Fewest Pieces Rule (URG Unit 4 & Unit 6; SG Unit 4)
Using the least number of base-ten pieces to represent a number. (*See also* base-ten pieces.)

Flat (URG Unit 4; SG Unit 4)
A block that measures 1 cm $\times$ 10 cm $\times$ 10 cm. It is one of the base-ten pieces that is often used to represent 100. (*See also* base-ten pieces.)

Flip (URG Unit 12)
A motion of the plane in which a figure is reflected over a line so that any point and its image are the same distance from the line.

Fraction (URG Unit 15)
A number that can be written as $\frac{a}{b}$ where a and b are whole numbers and b is not zero. For example, $\frac{1}{2}$, 0.5, and 2 are all fractions since 0.5 can be written as $\frac{5}{10}$ and 2 can be written as $\frac{2}{1}$.

Front-End Estimation (URG Unit 6)
Estimation by looking at the left-most digit.

G

Gallon (gal) (URG Unit 16)
A unit of volume equal to four quarts.

Gram
The basic unit used to measure mass.

H

Hexagon (SG Unit 12)
A six-sided polygon.

Horizontal Axis (SG Unit 1)
In a coordinate grid, the *x*-axis. The axis that extends from left to right.

I

Interpolation (URG Unit 7)
Making predictions or estimating values that lie between data points in a set of data.

J

K

Kilogram
1000 grams.

L

Likely Event (SG Unit 1)
An event that has a high probability of occurring.

Line of Symmetry (URG Unit 12)
A line is a line of symmetry for a plane figure if, when the figure is folded along this line, the two parts match exactly.

Line Symmetry (URG Unit 12; SG Unit 12)
A figure has line symmetry if it has at least one line of symmetry.

Liter (l) (URG Unit 16; SG Unit 16)
Metric unit used to measure volume. A liter is a little more than a quart.

M

Magic Square (URG Unit 2)
A square array of digits in which the sums of the rows, columns, and main diagonals are the same.

Making a Ten (URG Unit 2)
Strategies for addition and subtraction that make use of knowing the sums to ten. For example, knowing $6 + 4 = 10$ can be helpful in finding $10 - 6 = 4$ and $11 - 6 = 5$.

Mass (URG Unit 9 & Unit 16; SG Unit 9)
The amount of matter in an object.

Mean (URG Unit 5)
An average of a set of numbers that is found by adding the values of the data and dividing by the number of values.

Measurement Division (URG Unit 7)
Division as equal grouping. The total number of objects and the number of objects in each group are known. The number of groups is the unknown. For example, tulip bulbs come in packages of 8. If 216 bulbs are sold, how many packages are sold?

Measurement Error (URG Unit 9)
The unavoidable error that occurs due to the limitations inherent to any measurement instrument.

Median (URG Unit 5; DAB Unit 5)
For a set with an odd number of data arranged in order, it is the middle number. For an even number of data arranged in order, it is the number halfway between the two middle numbers.

Meniscus (URG Unit 16; SG Unit 16)
The curved surface formed when a liquid creeps up the side of a container (for example, a graduated cylinder).

Meter (m)
The standard unit of length measure in the metric system. One meter is approximately 39 inches.

Milliliter (ml) (URG Unit 16; SG Unit 16)
A measure of capacity in the metric system that is the volume of a cube that is one centimeter long on each edge.

Multiple (URG Unit 3 & Unit 11)
A number is a multiple of another number if it is evenly divisible by that number. For example, 12 is a multiple of 2 since 2 divides 12 evenly.

N

Numerator (URG Unit 13)
The number written above the line in a fraction. For example, the 2 is the numerator in the fraction $\frac{2}{3}$. (*See also* denominator.)

O

One-Dimensional Object (URG Unit 18; SG Unit 18)
An object is one-dimensional if it is made up of pieces of lines and curves.

Ordered Pairs (URG Unit 8)
A pair of numbers that gives the coordinates of a point on a grid in relation to the origin. The horizontal coordinate is given first; the vertical coordinate is given second. For example, the ordered pair (5, 3) tells us to move five units to the right of the origin and 3 units up.

Origin (URG Unit 8)
The point at which the *x*- and *y*-axes (horizontal and vertical axes) intersect on a coordinate plane. The origin is described by the ordered pair (0, 0) and serves as a reference point so that all the points on the plane can be located by ordered pairs.

P

Pack (URG Unit 4; SG Unit 4)
A cube that measures 10 cm on each edge. It is one of the base-ten pieces that is often used to represent 1000. (*See also* base-ten pieces.)

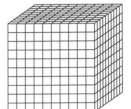

Palindrome (URG Unit 6)
A number, word, or phrase that reads the same forward and backward, e.g., 12321.

Parallel Lines (URG Unit 18)
Lines that are in the same direction. In the plane, parallel lines are lines that do not intersect.

Parallelogram (URG Unit 18)
A quadrilateral with two pairs of parallel sides.

Partitive Division (URG Unit 7)
Division as equal sharing. The total number of objects and the number of groups are known. The number of objects in each group is the unknown. For example, Frank has 144 marbles that he divides equally into 6 groups. How many marbles are in each group?

Pentagon (SG Unit 12)
A five-sided, five-angled polygon.

Perimeter (URG Unit 7; DAB Unit 7)
The distance around a two-dimensional shape.

Pint (URG Unit 16)
A unit of volume measure equal to 16 fluid ounces, i.e., two cups.

Polygon
A two-dimensional connected figure made of line segments in which each endpoint of every side meets with an endpoint of exactly one other side.

Population (URG Unit 1; SG Unit 1)
A collection of persons or things whose properties will be analyzed in a survey or experiment.

Prediction (SG Unit 1)
Using data to declare or foretell what is likely to occur.

Prime Number (URG Unit 11)
A number that has exactly two factors. For example, 7 has exactly two distinct factors, 1 and 7.

Prism
A three-dimensional figure that has two congruent faces, called bases, that are parallel to each other, and all other faces are parallelograms.

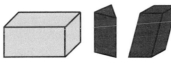

Prisms   Not a prism

Product (URG Unit 11; SG Unit 11; DAB Unit 11)
The answer to a multiplication problem. In the problem $3 \times 4 = 12$, 12 is the product.

Q

Quadrilateral (URG Unit 18)
A polygon with four sides.

Quart (URG Unit 16)
A unit of volume equal to 32 fluid ounces; one quarter of a gallon.

R

Recording Sheet (URG Unit 4)
A place value chart used for addition and subtraction problems.

Rectangular Prism (URG Unit 18; SG Unit 18)
A prism whose bases are rectangles. A right rectangular prism is a prism having all faces rectangles.

Regular (URG Unit 7; DAB Unit 7)
A polygon is regular if all sides are of equal length and all angles are equal.

Remainder (URG Unit 7)
Something that remains or is left after a division problem. The portion of the dividend that is not evenly divisible by the divisor, e.g., $16 \div 5 = 3$ with 1 as a remainder.

Right Angle (SG Unit 12)
An angle that measures 90°.

Rotation (turn) (URG Unit 12)
A transformation (motion) in which a figure is turned a specified angle and direction around a point.

Row (URG Unit 11)
In an array, the objects lined up horizontally.

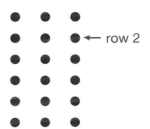

 ← row 2

Rubric (URG Unit 2)
A written guideline for assigning scores to student work, for the purpose of assessment.

S

Sample (URG Unit 1; SG Unit 1)
A part or subset of a population.

Skinny (URG Unit 4; SG Unit 4)
A block that measures 1 cm $\times$ 1 cm $\times$ 10 cm. It is one of the base-ten pieces that is often used to represent 10. (*See also* base-ten pieces.)

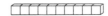

Square Centimeter (sq cm) (SG Unit 5)
The area of a square that is 1 cm long on each side.

Square Number (SG Unit 11)
A number that is the product of a whole number multiplied by itself. For example, 25 is a square number since $5 \times 5 = 25$. A square number can be represented by a square array with the same number of rows as columns. A square array for 25 has 5 rows of 5 objects in each row or 25 total objects.

Standard Masses
A set of objects with convenient masses, usually 1 g, 10 g, 100 g, etc.

Sum (URG Unit 2; SG Unit 2)
The answer to an addition problem.

Survey (URG Unit 14; SG Unit 14)
An investigation conducted by collecting data from a sample of a population and then analyzing it. Usually surveys are used to make predictions about the entire population.

T

Tangrams (SG Unit 12)
A type of geometric puzzle. A shape is given and it must be covered exactly with seven standard shapes called tans.

Thinking Addition (URG Unit 2)
A strategy for subtraction that uses a related addition problem. For example, $15 - 7 = 8$ because $8 + 7 = 15$.

Three-Dimensional (URG Unit 18; SG Unit 18)
Existing in three-dimensional space; having length, width, and depth.

TIMS Laboratory Method (URG Unit 1; SG Unit 1)
A method that students use to organize experiments and investigations. It involves four components: draw, collect, graph, and explore. It is a way to help students learn about the scientific method.

Turn (URG Unit 12)
(*See* rotation.)

Turn-Around Facts (URG Unit 2 & Unit 11 p. 37; SG Unit 11)
Addition facts that have the same addends but in a different order, e.g., $3 + 4 = 7$ and $4 + 3 = 7$. (*See also* commutative property of addition and commutative property of multiplication.)

Two-Dimensional (URG Unit 18; SG Unit 18)
Existing in the plane; having length and width.

Two-Pan Balance
A device for measuring the mass of an object by balancing the object against a number of standard masses (usually multiples of 1 unit, 10 units, and 100 units, etc.).

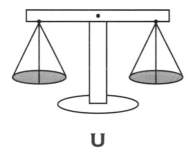

U

Unit (of measurement) (URG Unit 18)
A precisely fixed quantity used to measure. For example, centimeter, foot, kilogram, and quart are units of measurement.

Using a Ten (URG Unit 2)
1. A strategy for addition that uses partitions of the number 10. For example, one can find $8 + 6$ by thinking $8 + 6 = 8 + 2 + 4 = 10 + 4 = 14$.
2. A strategy for subtraction that uses facts that involve subtracting 10. For example, students can use $17 - 10 = 7$ to learn the "close fact" $17 - 9 = 8$.

Using Doubles (URG Unit 2)
Strategies for addition and subtraction that use knowing doubles. For example, one can find $7 + 8$ by thinking $7 + 8 = 7 + 7 + 1 = 14 + 1 = 15$. Knowing $7 + 7 = 14$ can be helpful in finding $14 - 7 = 7$ and $14 - 8 = 6$.

V

Value (URG Unit 1; SG Unit 1)
The possible outcomes of a variable. For example, red, green, and blue are possible values for the variable *color*. Two meters and 1.65 meters are possible values for the variable *length*.

Variable (URG Unit 1; SG Unit 1)
1. An attribute or quantity that changes or varies.
2. A symbol that can stand for a variable.

Vertex (URG Unit 12; SG Unit 12)
1. A point where the sides of a polygon meet.
2. A point where the edges of a three-dimensional object meet.

Vertical Axis (SG Unit 1)
In a coordinate grid, the *y*-axis. It is perpendicular to the horizontal axis.

Volume (URG Unit 16; SG Unit 16)
The measure of the amount of space occupied by an object.

Volume by Displacement (URG Unit 16)
A way of measuring volume of an object by measuring the amount of water (or some other fluid) it displaces.

W

Weight (URG Unit 9)
A measure of the pull of gravity on an object. One unit for measuring weight is the pound.

X

Y

Z